Ansible for VMware by Examples

A Step-by-Step Guide to Automating Your VMware Infrastructure

Luca Berton

apress®

Ansible for VMware by Examples: A Step-by-Step Guide to Automating Your VMware Infrastructure

Luca Berton
Czechia, Czech Republic

ISBN-13 (pbk): 978-1-4842-8878-8   ISBN-13 (electronic): 978-1-4842-8879-5
https://doi.org/10.1007/978-1-4842-8879-5

Managing Director, Apress Media LLC: Welmoed Spahr
Acquisitions Editor: Aditee Mirashi
Development Editor: James Markham
Coordinating Editor: Aditee Mirashi
Copy Editor: Mary Behr

Cover designed by eStudioCalamar

Cover image designed by Freepik (www.freepik.com)

Distributed to the book trade worldwide by Springer Science+Business Media New York, 1 New York Plaza, Suite 4600, New York, NY 10004-1562, USA. Phone 1-800-SPRINGER, fax (201) 348-4505, e-mail orders-ny@ springer-sbm.com, or visit www.springeronline.com. Apress Media, LLC is a California LLC and the sole member (owner) is Springer Science + Business Media Finance Inc (SSBM Finance Inc). SSBM Finance Inc is a **Delaware** corporation.

For information on translations, please e-mail booktranslations@springernature.com; for reprint, paperback, or audio rights, please e-mail bookpermissions@springernature.com.

Apress titles may be purchased in bulk for academic, corporate, or promotional use. eBook versions and licenses are also available for most titles. For more information, reference our Print and eBook Bulk Sales web page at www.apress.com/bulk-sales.

Any source code or other supplementary material referenced by the author in this book is available to readers on GitHub via the book's product page, located at www.apress.com/978-1-4842-8878-8. For more detailed information, please visit www.apress.com/source-code. You can also download the codes from GitHub at https://github.com/Apress/Ansible-for-VMware-by-Examples_Luca-Berton.

Printed on acid-free paper

For my son Filippo, the joy of my life.

Table of Contents

About the Author

Luca Berton is an Ansible Automation Expert who has been working with the Red Hat Ansible Engineer Team for three years. With more than 15 years of experience as a system administrator, he has strong expertise in infrastructure hardening and automation. An enthusiast of open source, he supports the community by sharing his knowledge in different events of public access. Geek by nature, Linux by choice, Fedora of course.

About the Technical Reviewer

Nikhil Jain is an Ansible expert with over 12 years of DevOps experience. He has been using Ansible and contributing to it from its inception. He currently works closely with Ansible Engineering.

He is an open source enthusiast and is part of the Ansible Pune Meetup Organizing team. He has presented multiple Ansible sessions at various global and local events. Apart from sitting in front of his computer automating things using Ansible, he loves watching sports and is a regular part of the local cricket team.

Acknowledgments

To my son, family, and friends who make life worth living and whose support and encouragement makes this work possible.

I'd like to thank my technical reviewer, Nikhil Jain, previously a Red Hat colleague, who joined my effort early on and contributed to the project.

To everyone I've worked with over the years and shared any ideas for this book: thank you for the knowledge you've shared.

Preface

This book is a guide to automating your VMware infrastructure using the Ansible open source technology.

If you are an IT professional in information technology in any industry and you would like a jargon-free understanding of Ansible technology, including VMware, Linux, and Windows Systems Administrators, DevOps professionals, thought leaders, Infrastructure-as-Code enthusiasts, and information technology team members providing leadership to a business, this book is for you.

This book can be a powerful resource for computer engineers and leaders who believe that innovation, automation, and acceleration are drivers for a successful business of tomorrow. Look back on your career path and think of at least three times a lack of infrastructure automation has been a challenge for your project's deadline. Remember the human errors that impacted your business continuity and then think of when effective infrastructure performance enabled your projects to succeed.

Consider the need for business and information technology departments and get curious about what that means for information technology and business stakeholders.

A successful infrastructure is a matter of gradual improvements and good habits that you can achieve by using more automation on your journey.

Learn how to become more productive and effective using the Ansible open source automation technology.

Engineers have great impact, power, and responsibility for the success of the business.

What Is In This Book?

This book provides in-depth content on the following topics:

- The Ansible code language for beginners and experienced users via examples

- Ansible installation on the most common operating systems

- Troubleshooting of common errors

- Information on the latest releases of Ansible and ansible-core packages

- Ansible for VMware infrastructure code snippets and examples

Your Development Environment

This book does not require you to use a specific IDE. You need a simple base environment consisting of

- A common editor: terminal (VIM, Emacs, Nano, Pico, etc.) or GUI (VS Code, Atom, Geany, etc.)

- A workstation with Ansible or ansible-core packages

- VMware vSphere ESX, VMware vSphere ESXi, or VMware vSphere vCenter Server (for VMware-specific code

Additional Online Resource

Luca Berton maintains a popular website on Ansible development at www.ansiblepilot.com.

Introduction

I wrote this book to share with you how to automate tasks in your VMware infrastructure with Ansible. Ansible is rapidly ramping-up automation technology. It has become popular nowadays as an open-source IT infrastructure automation tool. You may have heard of technologies such as Puppet, Chef, and Terraform. What makes Ansible so successful is that it is free, portable, powerful, remarkably human readable, easy, and fun to use. Ansible has expanded to be very valuable in further use cases in production, acceptance, and testing (PAT) infrastructure design patterns under the categories of Provisioning, Configuration Management, Application Deployment, Continuous Deployment, Automation, and Orchestration. Especially in the post-pandemic world, we all live in an interconnected, fast-paced world driven by innovation and acceleration in technology. IT infrastructure is more than ever a key cornerstone in the innovation journey of every modern business corporation. A lot of enterprises already take advantage of the timesaving, error-avoiding, and auto-healing infrastructures permitted by modern IT automated infrastructure. In example after example I will show you the best way to simplify your VMware journey and get the best value from your Ansible code. Every IT department nowadays manages some resources on bare metal servers, virtual machines, the cloud, containers, and edge computing. And the demand is growing more and more year-over-year. In this book, you are going to learn how to enable Ansible to interact with your VMware infrastructures such as data centers, clusters, host systems, datastores, and virtual machines. For example, you can automate the creating, deleting, updating, and gathering of information for virtual machines. Say goodbye to mundane and annoying manual activity and focus your effort on how to scale your infrastructure and enable your business for the challenges of tomorrow!

For all of you who are security paranoid, Ansible provides out-of-the-box support protection for sensitive data. For example, you store credentials and tokens in an Ansible Vault using at least the AES-256 security cipher.

Are you ready to automate your day with Ansible?

Some interesting resources to explore for a deep dive into the Ansible product:

- Official Ansible documentation, `https://docs.ansible.com/`

- Wikipedia Ansible page, `https://en.wikipedia.org/wiki/Ansible_ (software)`

Who Is This Book For?

This book is designed for IT professionals in the information technology industry who would like a jargon-free understanding of Ansible technology for automating a VMware infrastructure.

This book offers systems administrators, developers, DevOps, decision makers, and thought leaders a guideline about implementing Infrastructure-as-Code in your VMware infrastructure.

This book is designed for beginners of Ansible technology and is a great companion to intermediate and expert levels to the state-of-the-art of the Ansible platform.

The already experienced Ansible users are going to love the unique, specific code samples and examples for the Ansible for VMware infrastructure.

You are going to learn how to save time and avoid human errors by efficiently automating your VMware infrastructure using the Ansible open source IT automation technology enabling IaC for DevOps methodologies.

You can read this book with two different mindsets: development and operations. Both mindsets are going to love the practical approach of code snippets and code nutshells to easily apply to your day-to-day journey and challenges.

Many of the IT engineers I work with are already familiar with administering a fleet of Linux servers and are comfortable interacting via the OpenSSH protocol using command-line commands. These users use the so-called "imperative" programming to interact with machines. The Ansible platform evolves your fleet management as a declarative programming language so people already familiar with configuration management tools (Puppet or Chef) can find some connecting dots.

Modern IT Infrastructure

Deploying and managing applications requires more and more server machines that are reliable and efficient. Traditionally, system administrators took care of this burden for the internal (developers) and external (users) stakeholders who interact with the systems.

The day-to-day tasks of a system administrator involved the manual installation of software, changing of configurations, and management of services on servers, virtual machines, and nodes. And every day the IT department received requests to boost the data center's resources in order to accommodate the business needs or better tackle the marketplace. System administrators realized they couldn't scale their manual systems management scripts as fast as the business stakeholders demanded: the hosted web applications increased the complexity, email flow increased, and new releases of the operating systems continued. API-driven server management and configuration management tools like Ansible helped make things manageable for a time.

You could see this trend in the rise of the application-as-service, developer-centric methodologies DevOps and DevSecOps. Microservices, and serverless application architecture meant that a more seismic shift was coming. Instead of thinking in terms of servers and infrastructure, developers expect to be able to manage containerized application lifecycles, with no regard for the servers on which their applications run.

Modern business applications require one or more of the following features:

- Self-healing infrastructure
- Auto-scaling/elasticity
- High availability with multi-server failover
- Flexible or multi-tier storage backends
- Multi-cloud compatibility
- Enabling DevSecOps

The containerized app development and deployment became more and more popular with a huge number of technologies to real-time check these boxes, like Apache Mesos and Docker Swarm. Some cloud vendors even built their container orchestration and management products to meet the needs of cloud-native applications. Examples: Amazon Elastic Container Service (Amazon ECS) by Amazon Web Services (AWS), Google Container Engine (GKE) by Google Cloud Platform (GCP), Azure Container

Service by Microsoft Azure, IBM Bluemix Cloud Kubernetes Container Service by IBM Cloud, Oracle Container Cloud Service (OCCS) by Oracle Cloud, and Alibaba Cloud Container Registry.

Creative software engineers and solution creators love to use the Ansible Automation Platform (formerly Ansible Tower). It is the enterprise product used to store resources across your team and trigger automation recipes and workflows in the DevSecOps environment. Other popular tools like Jenkins, Rundeck, GitHub Actions, GitLab CI/CD, Atlassian Bamboo, CircleCI, TeamCity, Travis CI, BuildMaster, Bitrise, Buddy, or Go CI may also be used to enable continuous integration and continuous deployment in your organization.

Author Bio

I'm Luca Berton and we're going to have a lot of fun together.

I've been an Ansible expert and working directly with the Ansible Engineering Team of Red Hat for three years.

I have more than 15 years of system administration experience, working with infrastructures either on-premises or with the major cloud providers and technologies.

I'm an enthusiast of open source and I support the community by sharing my knowledge in different events of public access.

I'm also a co-founder of the FSUG Padova, my hometown Linux Users Group, visited by Richard Stallman, the founder of the Free Software Movement in 2007.

I consider myself a lazy person, so I always try new ways to automate the repetitive task of my work.

After years of Perl, Bash, and Python scripting, I landed on the Ansible technology. I took the certification and worked for more than three years with the Ansible Engineer Team.

I consider Ansible the best infrastructure automation technology nowadays. It's human-readable, the learning curve is accessible, and it is very requested by the recruiters in the market.

On every page of this book, I'm going to share with you one specific use case, the possible solution, the code, the execution, and the verification of the target system. All these solutions are battle-tested and used by me in my everyday automation.

You can easily jump between lessons and review them as many times as you need.

Awards and Recognitions

Since 2021, I have shared my knowledge about Ansible in my Ansible Pilot project and it is gaining more traction among IT professionals every day.

Some major milestones:

- "Ansible Anwendertreffen - From Zero to Hero: How to build the Ansible Pilot Community" by Luca Berton (Red Hat CZ) 15:15 - 16:00 February 22, 2022

- Author of *Red Hat Ansible Playbook* included in RHSB-2021-009 Log4Shell trigger Remote Code Execution in log4j (CVE-2021-44228) January 12, 2022

- *The Ansible Bullhorn #41 - A Newsletter for the Ansible Developer Community*, January 7, 2022

- *The Ansible Bullhorn #34 - A Newsletter for the Ansible Developer Community*, September 17, 2021

Are you ready to have fun together?

Conventions Used in the Book

This is a practical book, so it's jam-packed with code to be used on the command line plus commands and Ansible language code samples.

You are going to find commands and code samples throughout the book either inline (for example, `ansible [command]`), or in a code block (with or without line numbers) like

```
---
# YAML file example
```

The command-line commands use the standard POSIX conventions and are ready to be used in a Unix-like system such as Linux, macOS, or BSD. Each of the commands is assumed to be used by a standard user account when the prefix is the $ (dollar) symbol, or by the `root` user when the prefix is the # (number sign) symbol. You are going to find this code in some installation, code execution, and troubleshooting examples. The commands were tested in the most used Linux distributions on the market nowadays.

The Ansible language code, used in the Ansible Playbook examples, mostly uses the YAML and INI formats.

The YAML format, a human-readable, data-serialization language, is extremely popular nowadays for configuration files. The code follows the latest YAML 1.2.2 specification. It uses Python-style indentation and a more compact format for lists and dictionary statements. It's very close to JSON and can be used as an XML alternative. The YAML code was validated using the YAMLlint popular validator and tested in the most used Ansible versions out in the market nowadays.

The INI format used in some Ansible Inventory examples is a well-known format for configuration files since the MS-DOS operating system and uses key-value pairs for properties.

The Ansible code included in this book was tested by the author and the technical reviewer in a wide variety of modern systems and uses the Ansible best practices about Playbooks, Roles, and Collections. It was verified using the latest release of the Ansible Linter.

Some code may intentionally break a specific Ansible best practice rule only to demonstrate a troubleshooting session to reproduce a fatal error in a specific use case.

Chapters at a Glance

This book is going to become a cornerstone on your journey through the Ansible platform for the VMware infrastructure. Although there are four chapters, the book is jam-packed with code samples and command-line commands that save time and avoid human mistakes enabling IaC for DevOps and DevSecOps methodologies.

Learn about the state-of-the-art Ansible platform today in Chapter 1. Concepts like inventories, Playbooks, tasks, common computer coding language statements concepts and code reuse, facts and magic variables, roles, and collections are explained and clarified as well as powerful key advantages such as idempotency.

Learn how to successfully install the Ansible platform on the most used modern operating systems in Chapter 2. Familiarize yourself with the Ansible community vs. ansible-core packages for the most used Linux distributions, macOS, and Windows.

Learn how to apply all this knowledge to the VMware infrastructure domain with specific Ansible Playbook code, such as how to upgrade VMware Guest Tools or move virtual machines between servers in Chapter 3.

CHAPTER 1

Ansible for Beginners with Examples

What are Ansible's basic concepts, architecture, and terminology? You are going to do a deep dive into Ansible jargon and take your first steps toward using the best open source automation technology on the market. If you're completely new to Ansible, this is the foundation of your journey. You'll learn the terminology used by automation professionals all around the world. If you already know something about Ansible, I'm sure that you are going to find some valuable information about Ansible automation and some recent changes in its release policies and tools.

This chapter provides a description of the Ansible technology and how to write and execute your first Ansible Playbook code.

What Is Ansible?

Let's begin with a short overview about what Ansible is and why it is so powerful.

Ansible was created more or less in February 2012 by Michael DeHaan, a brilliant employee of Red Hat at the time. Michael was inspired by several tools and his direct experience in the system administrator industry. There was a strong need for configuration management to enable the use of the same configuration across a Linux administrated fleet and the ability to consistently modify the config files every time. Michael started the Ansible tool in Python, the most interesting computer language at the time, and built the foundation of the module-based and agentless architecture. Every module performs a specific task and creates some Python bytecode that gets sent directly to the execution node via SSH for Linux, Unix (*BSD), and macOS targets. For Windows, target Ansible produces a PowerShell or CMD deliverable, shared via WinRM

© Luca Berton 2023
L. Berton, *Ansible for VMware by Examples*, https://doi.org/10.1007/978-1-4842-8879-5_1

to perform the expected outcome. This simple and extensible approach created the initial community. Michael created a company to support the initial demand and it was acquired by Red Hat in 2015. At the present time, Red Hat is leading the Ansible project and creating the roadmap for the Community and Enterprise deliverables of the Ansible project.

Ansible

- Infrastructure automation tool

- Open source Infrastructure-as-Code (IaC)

Let's begin this adventure with the fabulous open source technology named Ansible. It is classified as an infrastructure automation tool, so you can automate your system administrator tasks very easily.

Ansible enables in your enterprise a process called Infrastructure-as-Code, a way to processes the provisioning and managing of machines using simple human-readable definition files. This is extremely useful in a data center environment when the same task is commonly repeated among a bunch of machines. Before Ansible, manual configuration required complex and specialized technical people for hardware configuration and interactive configuration tools. Ansible lets you use DevOps methodology principles. This programming style is also called "declarative" because its focuses on the outcome of the execution and not on the single action such as in the traditional imperative programming languages (C, C++, Java, Python, etc.)

With Ansible, you can deploy your IaC on-premises and on the most well-known public cloud providers.

Three Main Use Cases

- Provisioning

- Configuration management

- Application deployment

The three main use cases of Ansible are provisioning, configuration management, and application deployment. But gaining an understanding of the technology I'm sure you can invent some more ways to use it!

Provisioning

- The process of setting up the IT infrastructure

Let's start talking about provisioning. All system administrators know how important it is to manage a uniform fleet of machines. Some people still rely on software to create workstation images. But there is a drawback because with imaging technology you're only taking a snapshot in time of the machine, so every time you need to reinstall software because of the modern key activation systems or update manually to the latest security patches. Ansible helps automate this process by create a smoother process.

Configuration Management

- The process of maintaining systems and software in a desired and consistent state

The second key use case is configuration management: maintaining an up-to-date and consistent way across your fleet of coordinating rolling updates and scheduling downtime. With Ansible, you can verify the status of your managed hosts and take action in a small group of them. A huge variety of modules is available for the most common use cases, including checking the compliance of your fleet to some international standards and applying resolution plans.

Application Deployment

- The process of publishing your software between testing, staging, and production environments

The third key use case where Ansible is useful is application deployment. It can automate the continuous integration/continuous delivery workflow pipeline of your web applications, for example. Your DevOps team will be delighted!.

Ansible For DevOps

Ansible is used to apply DevOps principles in worldwide organizations. Let me quickly summarize. The DevOps methodology consists of a very high-level set of best practices to follow in the full software lifecycle from the initial design, coding, testing, releasing, active use, and retirement from the market. These principles apply to small as well as to big projects and are used by today's IT professionals worldwide in small to large organizations. Generally speaking, it applies engineering principles to the software creation process. DevOps is so popular because has the following strengths: performance, reuse, repeatability, fault tolerance, and cost reduction. Also, the software used in a DevOps environment is defined as "toolchains" rather than a single command or tool. The toolchains are usually specifically designed for one specific task. A common way to classify them is using DevOps categories. Each category reflects the key aspect of the software design, development testing, and delivery process. The eight DevOps categories are

- **Plan**: The product/project manager analyzes the requirements and feedback from internal and external stakeholder and creates a product roadmap. The software is typically Jira, Azure DevOps, or Asana.

- **Code**: The development process that produces the code of your project. Toolchains vary based on the computer language used and source code versioning management tools.

- **Build**: These toolchains are very specific according to the computer language of your team. Methodologies of continuous integration/continuous deployment (CI/CD) and build status apply.

- **Test**: Continuous testing toolchains guarantee fast and updated results based on business risks often based on IaC and many DevOps pipelines.

- **Release**: A set of tools that packages your software in a repository.

- **Deploy**: The software enters the production phase. IaC to release in a two stages blue-green deployment to use new production services without any interruption of the service.

- **Operate**: Infrastructure configuration and management. Infrastructure scaling and acquisition of feedback about the service.

- **Monitor**: Application performance monitoring and end user experience feedback.

Four Key Tenets of Ansible

1. **Declarative:** You declare what you want rather than how to get to it.

2. **Agentless:** You don't need to install an agent. It takes advantage of OpenSSH.

3. **Idempotent:** An operation can be run multiple times without changing beyond the initial operation.

4. **Community driven:** Open source and extensible by Ansible Galaxy collections and roles.

The four key tenets of Ansible are declarative, agentless, idempotent, and community driven. With "declarative," it means that you can use it in a way very similar to a programming language to apply sequencing, selection, and iteration to the code flow. With "agentless," it means that Ansible operates in a way that doesn't require installing an all-active process (agent) on the target machine; it uses the SSH connection and a Python interpreter. For Linux and Unix machines, this means using SSH, either using OpenSSH or in constrained environments Paramiko (a Python OpenSSH library). For Windows hosts, this means using Windows Remote Management via PowerShell remoting.

The language itself is idempotent, which means that the code will check a precise status on the managed machine. It means that, for example, the first time it runs, your code will change something and the following runs only verify that nothing has changed and then it moves forward. The last tenet is "community driven," which means that Ansible is an open source technology. Moreover, there exists a public archive of extension resources called Ansible Galaxy where you can download code made by other open source contributors to extend it even more. This code is organized in roles and collections, and you'll see them later in this book.

Six Values of Ansible

- **Simple**: YAML human-readable automation

- **Powerful**: Configuration management, workflow orchestration, application deployment

- **Cross-platform**: Agentless support for all major OSes, physical, virtual, cloud, and network

- **Works with existing tools**: Homogenizes the existing environment

- **"Batteries included:"** 750+ modules available

- **Community powered**: Downloads of ~250k/month, ~3,500 contributors, 1,200 users on IRC

Now let's talk about the six values of Ansible. The first is that it is simple: the code is written in the YAML language, also known as a human-readable data serialization language. It is well known and easy to learn. It is very often used for configuration files of services, databases, and inside applications where data is stored or transmitted. Ansible is powerful. It is battle-tested in configuration management, workflow orchestration, and application deployment. The third value is that it's cross-platform by nature. It offers agentless support for all major operating systems, physical, virtual, cloud, and network providers. Another value of Ansible is that it works with existing IT tools, so it is easy to homogenize the existing environment. It's common to hear a success story about integration with popular DevOps or DevSecOps tools like Jenkins, Rundeck, GitHub Actions, GitLab CI/CD, Atlassian Bamboo, CircleCI, TeamCity, Travis CI, BuildMaster, Bitrise, Buddy, or Go CI might to enable CI/CD in your organization. The "batteries included" part means that Ansible has more than 750 modules currently available to automate most common tasks. These modules come out of the box via the Ansible community package and can be easily installed on top of the `ansible-core` platform. More details about Ansible packaging are in Chapter 2 of this book. The last value is that Ansible is community powered. Every month it has more than 250,000 downloads, an average of 3,500 contributors, and more than 1,200 users on IRC.

Ansible History

- 2012: Developed by Michael DeHaan

- 2015: Acquired by Red Hat

- 2016: AnsibleFest events

- 2020: Red Hat Ansible Automation Platform 1.0

- 2021: Red Hat Ansible Automation Platform 2.1

- 2022: Red Hat Ansible Automation Platform 2.2

Let's talk more about the main events in Ansible's history. The first release of Ansible was on February 20, 2012. Michael DeHaan created the Ansible tool and started advertising the first initial community. Later, he founded Ansible Inc. (initially AnsibleWorks Inc.), which guaranteed the commercial support and sponsorship of the project. On October 16, 2015, Ansible Inc. was acquired by Red Hat, which evaluated Ansible as a "powerful IT automation solution." This is great recognition for the Ansible technology that everyday helps enterprises innovate in the IT industry. Every year since 2016, the Ansible Community reunites at an event called AnsibleFest (virtually during pandemic time) with conferences for users and contributors all around the planet.

Ansible, Ansible Tower, and the Ansible Automation Platform

- Ansible

Community-driven project with fast-moving innovations using the open source paradigm but only command line tools.

- Red Hat Ansible Tower/Ansible Automation Platform

A framework designed by RedHat. It provides a web UI to manage your infrastructure.

Ansible is an open source, community-driven project with fast-moving innovations but only command-line tools. Enterprise needs more services and some stable releases. For example, they need an SLA for support. Red Hat offers this service to companies under the Ansible Tower umbrella, now rebranded as Ansible Automation Platform. The Ansible Automation Platform includes Ansible Controller (previously known as Ansible Tower) and Automation Hub. Ansible Controller offers an easy-to-use web user interface as a way to organize the automation needs of your organization. It also offers a REST API and web services. It is designed to form more than a one-person IT department and teams that need to share processes and sensitive data. It also provides role-based access control (RBAC) to easily assign based on your team's needs and skill sets. It is the center of all the automation tasks and jobs operations. Red Hat also releases the open source part of the Ansible Controller called AWX project, the upstream project of Ansible Tower, available since September 2017. Red Hat also maintains Ansible Core (previously known as Ansible Engine). Ansible Core is the milestone that contains the Ansible platform, language, and tools to succeed in your automation journey. Red Hat provides commercial support for the enterprise customers of these products as well as the project roadmap for the community.

Getting Started

It's time to take your first step with Ansible technology. You'll learn how to connect to the managed hosts and how to execute some simple tasks using the Ansible command line tool.

Ansible Architecture

Let's begin by talking about the Ansible architecture. The node where Ansible is actually installed is called the Ansible **control node** and it manages your fleet of nodes. The controlled node is called a **managed node** or **target node**. The target node could be Linux, Mac, Windows, or network equipment. Each target has some specificity like different Linux distributions and module usage. We will discuss the specificity in the next sections.

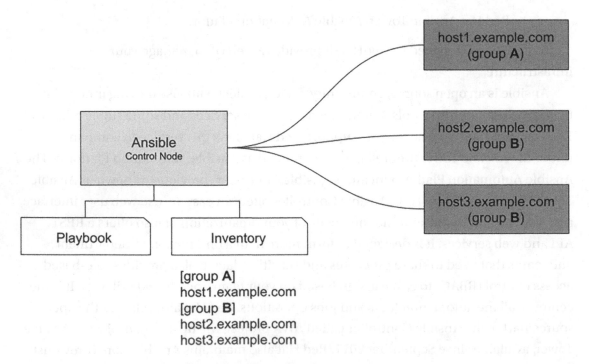

Figure 1-1. *Ansible architecture schema*

Connecting with Managed Nodes

The connection between the control node and managed nodes is managed by the SSH protocol without any requirement for a specific client on the Linux/Unix target machine. Other competitors require client software often called an agent. With an SSH connection, the only requirements are a username and a public/private OpenSSH key to access the target machine. There are some ways to automate this first script step. After completing the SSH connection, another requirement is a Python interpreter, which comes out of the box for modern operating systems. Ansible uses the SSH connection in SFTP/SCP mode to transfer files between the control and target nodes. The Windows target is connected with the WinRM technology and uses PowerShell as an interpreter by default, but you can also choose CMD.

In Ansible 2.8+ you can also use OpenSSH with Windows but it's still a limited option.

Ansible Installation

The Ansible installation on the control node is covered in Chapter 2 of this book.

Creating a Basic Inventory

- /etc/ansible/hosts

  demo.example.com

- default inventory file /etc/ansible/hosts

  demo.example.com is a managed host

The list of managed hosts is stored in /etc/ansible/hosts, specifying the hostname of the IP addresses. In this example, it contains only one host named demo.example.com that resolves in your local DNSF or more inventory options such as a static IP address, username, connection type, and SSH key path. Refer to the host variables section in the following chapter.

Running Your First Ansible Command

The ping command is your first Ansible command. It simply interacts with the target node and returns a "pong" status when successful. Once Ansible is successfully installed (see Chapter 2) on your Ansible control node, you can use the Ansible command line tool from your favorite terminal application. The name of the terminal application might vary based on your operating system (Linux/Mac/Windows) but the parameters and output of the Ansible command are always the same. The command result status could be SUCCESS, CHANGED, SKIPPED, OK, and FAILED. The SUCCESS status means successful execution of the command and no modification performed on the target machine. The CHANGED status means successful execution of the command and some changes performed on the target node. The SKIPPED status means some condition doesn't permit the execution of the task on the target node (usually a when statement). The OK status means an idempotent result on the module, the changes are already present in the target node, or the module interacts in read-only mode in the target node. The FAILED status means some error during the execution of the command or communication with the target node; usually more details are provided in a descriptive message.

This is your first Ansible command:

```
$ ansible all -m ping
```

- ping module executed on all hosts

- demo.example.com replied with a success code

The output includes

- Target host: demo.example.com

- Command result: SUCCESS

- Return value:

    "ping": "pong"

Each Ansible command is called also a **module** in Ansible jargon. The first line executed the Ansible **ping** module on all hosts. The response is a pong. Please note that this means that Ansible is able to connect with the SSH username, identify it using the public key, and execute the local Python executer. So, it's completely different from any ping in networking.

Running Ad-Hoc Commands on Ansible

```
$ ansible all -a '/bin/echo example'
```

The output includes

- Command result: CHANGED

- Return value:

example

- /bin/echo example command executed on all hosts

- demo.example.com replied with a changed code and print example on the standard output

Ansible can also execute commands on the target host and report the status on the console of the Ansible control node. In this example, the /bin/echo example command was executed on all hosts. demo.example.com replied with a changed code and printed the example text on the standard output. You can substitute the echo with printf bash command for Linux systems. Note that every time the Ansible module alters any configuration on the target machine, you will receive a changed Ansible status in return.

Running Ad-Hoc Commands with Privilege Escalation on Ansible

```
$ ansible all -m ping -u devops --become
```

The output includes

- Command result: SUCCESS

- Return value:

  "ping": "pong"

- ping module executed on all host as user root after login with user devops

- demo.example.com replied with a changed code and print "ping": "pong" on the standard output

In this example, you run the `ping` module against the `all` host as user `root` after a login with user `devops`. `demo.example.com` replies with a changed code and prints "ping": "pong" on standard output.

Recap

In this section, you learned the basic concept of the Ansible architecture, how to write a list of managed hosts, and how to execute some simple commands against it.

Inventory

In this section, I'll explain what an Ansible Inventory is, why you need it, the different types, and how to edit and use it in your day-to-day journey.

- An inventory is the set of hosts Ansible can work against.
- They can be categorized as groups/patterns.

The list of multiple hosts managed by Ansible is called an inventory. An Ansible inventory is fundamentally a list of target hosts to execute your automation against. The target hosts can be in the same or different infrastructure(s). The hosts can be organized in one or more groups or patterns in order to filter hosts according to common criteria.

- `all` keyword

The keyword `all` includes all hosts of the inventory, except localhost. The special keyword `all` includes all the hosts of the inventory used. It will be very useful in the following lessons. The only exception is localhost, which you need to specify.

Simple INI Inventory

- `./ini_simple_inventory`

    `host1.example.com`

    `[frontends]`
    `host2.example.com`
    `host3.example.com`

- file name: `ini_simple_inventory`

- host1.example.com is ungrouped

- host2.example.com and host3.example.com are grouped as frontends

The simplest inventory type is the INI inventory, by the type of the file stored by default in /etc/ansible/hosts. You can specify a customized Ansible inventory using the -i parameter in your ansible or ansible-playbook terminal. In this example, host host1.example.com is ungrouped but host2.example.com and host3.example.com are grouped as frontends.

Simple YAML Inventory

You can express the same inventory using the YAML syntax.

- ./simple_yaml_inventory.yml

```
---
all:
  hosts:
    host1.example.com:
  children:
    frontends:
      hosts:
        host2.example.com:
        host3.example.com:
```

- file name: inventory.yml

- host1.example.com is ungrouped

- host2.example.com and host3.example.com are grouped as frontends

In this example, the host host1.example.com is ungrouped, but host2.example.com and host3.example.com are grouped as frontends.

Adding Ranges of Hosts

Group members can be defined also using ranges by numbers or letters.

- ./ini_range_inventory

  ```
  [frontends]
  www[01:99].example.com
  ```

  ```
  [backends]
  back-[a-f].example.com
  ```

- The frontends group contains all hosts from www01.example.com to www99.example.com.

- The backends group contains all hosts from back-a.example.com to back-f.example.com.

In the range by numbers, you can also specify a stride as the increment between a sequence of numbers. In this INI example, the frontends group contains all hosts from www01.example.com to www99.example.com. The backends group contains all hosts from back-a.example.com to back-f.example.com.

Hosting in Multiple Groups

Hosts can be present in multiple groups.

- ./ini_groupsmultiple_inventory

  ```
  host1.example.com
  ```

  ```
  [frontends]
  host2.example.com
  host3.example.com
  ```

  ```
  [prod]
  host2.example.com
  ```

  ```
  [dev]
  host3.example.com
  ```

- hosts host2.example.com and host3.example.com are present in multiple groups.

In this INI example, hosts host2.example.com and host3.example.com are grouped as frontends. The host host2.example.com is present in the frontends as well as the prod group. The host host3.example.com is present in both frontends and dev groups.

Host Variables

In an inventory, you may want to store values as variables and associate them with a specific host or group.

- ./ini_hostinventory

```
[frontends]
localhost  ansible_connection=local
host1.example.com ansible_connection=ssh ansible_user=devops
host2.example.com ansible_connection=ssh ansible_user=ansible
host3.example.com ansible_user=example ansible_ssh_private_key_
file=~/prj/id_rsa
host4.example.com ansible_host=10.0.113.111
```

- ansible_connection and ansible_user customized variables

This example scenario is very common because it defines different connections with different hosts. For example, use local connection for the localhost and ssh, the default, for all the other hosts. For each host, you can also customize the login user devops for host1.example.com and ansible for host2.example.com. The host host3.example.com authenticates with the user example with a custom SSH key path. The host host4.example.com has an inventory-defined static IP address. This means that Ansible resolves the host4.example.com with 10.0.113.111.

Group Variables

Group variables enable you to assign variables to a specific group defined in an Ansible inventory.

- ./groupsvariables_inventory_ini

```
[frontends]
host1.example.com
```

```
        host2.example.com

        [frontends:vars]
        ntp_server=europe.pool.ntp.org
```

- ./groupsvariables_inventory_yaml.yml

```
---
frontends:
  hosts:
    host2.example.com:
    host3.example.com:
  vars:
    ntp_server: europe.pool.ntp.org
```

It is extremely useful not to repeat the same value for a lot of target nodes, for example for the same NTP server for all your host in your network. In the two inventory files in the example (INI and YAML formats), the variable ntp_server assigned the value europe.pool.ntp.org for all the hosts of the group.

Inheriting Variable Values

Hosts and groups can be combined.

- ./ini_variableinheriting_inventory

```
[asia]
host1.example.com

[europe]
host2.example.com

[frontends:children]
asia
europe

[frontends:vars]
ntp_server=europe.pool.ntp.org
```

- ./variableinheriting_inventory.yml

```
---
children:
  frontends:
    children:
      asia:
        hosts:
          host1.example.com:
      europe:
        hosts:
          host2.example.com:
    vars:
      ntp_server: europe.pool.ntp.org
```

In this example, the group frontends has two members, asia and europe. These two groups contain only a single host each, host1.example.com and host2.example. com, respectively, but can contain more hosts. The variable ntp_server is defined at the frontends level. So, in the end, the ntp_server variable is visible in all three groups: frontends, asia, and europe. The host1.example.com and host2.example.com hosts inherit the ntp_server variable from their related groups.

Using Multiple Inventory Sources

It is possible to use multiple inventory files for each execution.

```
$ ansible-playbook -i production -i development playbook.yml
```

- Execute the Ansible Playbook named playbook.yml against the production and development inventories.

This example executes the Ansible Playbook named playbook.yml against the production and development inventories.

The localhost Inventory

One special case in inventory is with the `localhost` host.

- `./ini_local_inventory`

  `localhost ansible_connection="local"`

- File name: `inventory`

- `/etc/ansible/hosts` default

You need to specify the connection type as `local`; otherwise, Ansible presumes to use the default SSH connection. It's very common to also specify the Python interpreter, as mentioned in the `ansible_python_interpreter: "{{ansible_playbook_python}}"`.

Recap

Now you know more about Ansible INI and YAML inventory files to specify target hosts of your automation as well as variables with parameters that affected your execution.

Playbook

In this section, I'll explain what an Ansible Playbook is and why you need it. I'll cover how to start with a simple Playbook from the basic syntax and how to add more tasks.

A playbook is a set of plays to be executed against an inventory.

YAML Syntax

```
# A sample YAML comment
statement # Another YAML comment

A sample string
'Another string'
"Another string"

with_newlines: |
Example Enterprise
813 Howard Street Oswego
```

```
New York, NY 13126

without_newlines: >
This is an example
of a long string,
that will become
a single sentence.

yaml_dictionary: {name1: value1, name2: value2}

yaml_list1:
- value1
- value2
yaml_list2: [value1, value2]
```

Every Playbook is based on YAML syntax so the file is easy and human readable. YAML is a text format, and you can easily recognize it by the presence of the three dash symbols at the beginning and three dots at the end. The three dots are not mandatory, so a lot of people omit them. This file type is very sensitive to spacing between elements. It's strictly important that elements of the same level are in the same indentation, unlike in some programming languages. You can use the symbol # for comments, even on lines with previous code. A string is very important and you can specify it directly or with a single or double quotes. I recommend using double quotes as a general rule. Using the pipe and major statement you can define multi-line strings. The first statement keeps the newlines, the second does not. Other useful data structures are dictionaries and lists, which you can see in action on the grayboard.

helloworld.yml

- helloworld.yml

```
---
- name: message demo
  hosts: all
  tasks:
    - name: sample message
      ansible.builtin.debug:
        msg: "Sample Text"
```

```
...
file name: helloworld.yml
Name of the playbook: "message demo"
Hosts of execution: "all"
List of tasks
One task named "sample message"
Module ansible.builtin.debug
Argument `msg` of module debug
```

This is the output of the execution of the `helloworld.yml`. Note that the command used is `ansible-playbook`. The first parameter is the inventory file and the second is the Playbook. In this execution, the play is executed against the `host1.example.com` node. The output is very clear by the step-by-step execution. When the command is successful, the output is highlighted with a green color. A warning is presented in orange and an error in red. The most observant of you have noticed an extra task executed called `Gathering Facts`, which is performed by Ansible to acquire some information about the managed node. I'll discuss fact gathering in the following section. Try the execution of this code and become confident with this output summary. It will be very useful. Two tasks are being executed.

Tip 1: ansible-playbook —check Option

```
$ ansible-playbook -i inventory --check helloworld.yml
```

The output includes

- Target host: `demo.example.com`

- Command result: `ok=2`

- Return value:

  `Sample Text`

A very useful option is `--check` for Ansible Playbook commands. The Ansible Playbook will be executed in a sort of "dry run" mode. In this mode, Ansible *simulates* the execution on the target machine and reports each change but doesn't perform any actual action on the target machine. Not all Ansible modules support the **check mode**.

Tip 2: Debug Day-to-Day Usage

- `helloworld_debug.yml`

```
---
- name: message debug demo
  hosts: all
  tasks:
    - name: sample message
      ansible.builtin.debug:
        msg: "Sample Text"
        verbosity: 2
...
file name: helloworld_debug.yml
Name of the playbook: "message debug demo"
Hosts of execution: "all"
List of tasks
One task named "sample message"
Module debug
Argument `msg` of module debug
Argument `verbosity` is `2`
```

This tip allows you to keep the debug code in your Playbook and enable the execution only when you need it. For example, the message is printed only when Ansible is invoked with output level two.

- Execution without any verbose parameter

```
$ ansible-playbook -i inventory helloworld_debug.yml
```

The output includes

- Target host: `demo.example.com`

- Command result: `skipped=1`

- Return value:

```
skipping: [demo.example.com]
```

This is the output of `helloworld_debug.yml` when it is executed normally, which means not in debug mode. Note that the hello message is skipped.

- Execution with the verbose parameter

  ```
  $ ansible-playbook -i inventory -vv helloworld_debug.yml
  ```

The output includes

- Target host: `demo.example.com`

- Command result: `ok=2`

- Return value:

```
ok: [demo.example.com] => {
    "msg": "Sample Text"
}
```

This is the output of `helloworld_debug.yml` when it is executed in debug level two mode. Note the two `V` (like `Victor`) letters in the command line. And note that the hello message is printed.

Idempotency

One important characteristic of most Ansible modules is to be idempotent. It means that before executing any actions on the target node, the module checks the actual status. If the actual status matches the desired once, no action is performed. If the current status diverges from the expected one, an action will take place. Please note that if you execute the Playbook another time, the desired status will be found and no further actions will be performed. This property is called idempotency and you're going to take advantage of it.

multipleplays.yml

```
---
- name: first play
  hosts: www.example.com
  tasks:
    - name: first task
      ansible.builtin.yum:
```

```
          name: httpd
          status: present
      - name: second task
        ansible.builtin.service:
          name: httpd
          enabled: true
- name: second play
  hosts: database.example.com
  tasks:
      - name: first task
        ansible.builtin.service:
          name: mariadb
          enabled: true
```

- File name: multipleplays.yml. Two plays inside to be executed against web.example.com and database.example.com.

The multipleplays.yml Playbook contains two Ansible plays. In the beginning, the first Ansible play is executed against the target www.example.com host and installs an Apache web server and enables it on boot. The second play is executed against database.example.com and enables on boot the execution of the MariaDB database management system. As you can see, using multiple plays is a very powerful way to execute different tasks in different hosts. Now the definition of a Playbook makes more sense.

privilege_escalation.yml

```
---
- name: install httpd
  hosts: web.example.com
  become: true
  become_method: sudo
  become_user: root
  tasks:
      - name: install httpd
        ansible.builtin.yum:
          name: httpd
          status: present
```

- `privilege_escalation.yml` specifies that privilege escalation is necessary. The `become_method` specifies the escalation method. `become_user` specifies the destination user (default `root`).

Some action needs to be taken by a user with administrative power. In Linux, it's typically the `root` user. Some distributions allow for privilege escalation using the `sudo` command using the `wheel` group. The Ansible task will install the httpd Apache web server software so Ansible needs the root privilege to perform the task. This step is called "privilege escalation." The `yum` module needs to perform some action on the managed node. In the Playbook, when it is not necessary, you can disable it.

Common Ansible Modules

The most used Ansible modules included in the so-called "core" platform are listed under the builtin collection and are shipped with each version of Ansible.

- Files modules
  - `copy`: Copies files from a local file or directory to the managed host
  - `fetch`: Copies files from remote nodes to local files
  - `file`: Sets permissions and other properties of files
  - `lineinfile`: Adds or verifies that a particular line is or is not in a file configuration
  - `synchronize`: Synchronizes content using Rsync
- Software package modules
  - `package`: Manages packages using the autodetected package manager native to the operating system
  - `yum`: Manages packages using the YUM package manager
  - `apt`: Manages packages using the APT package manager
  - `dnf`: Manages packages using the DNF package manager
  - `gem`: Manages Ruby gems
  - `pip`: Manages Python packages from PyPI

- System modules

    - `firewalld`: Manages arbitrary ports and services using firewalld

    - `reboot`: Reboots a machine

    - `service`: Manages services

    - `user`: Adds, removes, and manages user accounts

- Net tools modules

    - `get_url`: Downloads files in HTTP, HTTPS, and FTP

    - `nmcli`: Manages networking

    - `uri`: Interacts with web services

Refer to the official Ansible website for the full list of modules included in the builtin collection available in the official website.

Refer also to the full list of modules divided by collections. Please note that modules in a collection might require an additional collection installation process.

Recap

In this section, you put the foundation of the following operation on an Ansible Playbook. Keep going and soon you will be able to automate all your system administrator tasks.

Variables

In this section, I'll explain what Ansible variables are, why you need them, the different types, and how to edit and use them in your day-to-day journey.

Variables store dynamic value for a given environment.

In your Playbook, it is a good practice to use variables to store all of the dynamic values that you need. By editing variables you can reuse your code in the future, only parameterized according to your business needs.

Not Permitted Variable Names

- No white spaces: `my var`

- No dots: `my.var`

- Don't start with a number: `1stvar`

- No special characters: `myvar$1`

Ansible allows combinations of letters and numbers in variable names. If you plan to use numbers, be aware that you can't use them at the beginning, but this is a general rule in the information technology world. The four main limitations in variable names are no white spaces are allowed, no dots, don't start with numbers, and don't use special characters. On the right are examples of invalid variable names.

variableprint.yml

- `./variableprint.yml`

```
---
- name: variable demo
  hosts: all
  vars:
    fruit: "apple"
  tasks:
    - name: print variable
      ansible.builtin.debug:
        msg: "The value of the variable {{ fruit }}"
file name: variableprint.yml
Name of the playbook: "variable demo"
Hosts of execution: "all"
List of tasks
One task named "print variable"
Module debug
Argument "msg" of module debug
```

The `variableprint.yml` Playbook is similar to the `helloworld.yml` Playbook. The syntax and the structure of the elements are very similar, except for the presence of the variable `fruit`. Variables store information like strings, numbers, and more complex data structures like lists, dictionaries, and such. In this case, the variable has the name `fruit` and the value `apple`. The debug module in this case will concatenate the text "The value of the variable" with the value of the `fruit` variable, "apple" in this example. Please note the double brackets, which means the value of the variable. It's a best practice always to include the double brackets within the double quote in the code.

- Execution

    ```
    $ ansible-playbook -i inventory variableprint.yml
    ```

The output includes

- Target host: `demo.example.com`

- Command result: `ok=2`

- Return value:

    ```
    ok: [demo.example.com] => {
        "msg": "The value of the variable apple"
    }
    ```

The output of the execution of `variableprint.yml` is very similar to that of the `helloworld.yml` file. Please note the printing of the message "The value of the variable apple," which is obtained by combining the string with the value of the variable. Also, this execution is successful, as you can see in the play recap area and by the green color. Two tasks are being executed.

variableprint.yml - Extra Variables

```
$ ansible-playbook -i inventory  -e fruit=banana  variableprint.yml
```

The output includes

- Target host: `demo.example.com`

- Command result: `ok=2`

- Return value:

```
ok: [demo.example.com] => {
    "msg": "The value of the variable banana"
}
```

You can override the Playbook variables to specify the value in the command line before the execution. When you set the variable value in this way, it is called an extra variable. This output of the execution of variableprint.yml is very similar to the previous one. Please note the printing of the message "The value of the variable banana," obtained by combining the string with the value of the variable. The value passed from the command line overrides any Playbook value.

Host Variables and Group Variables

- inventory_host_variables

```
[servers]
demo1.example.com ansible_user=devops
```

- inventory_group_variables

```
[servers]
demo1.example.com
demo2.example.com

[servers:vars]
user=alice
```

Host and group variables can be defined in your inventory file. In the left column, you see an example of a host variable. The variable ansible_user is assigned the value devops. This host variable is available for demo1.example.com. On the right column, you see an example of a group variable. The variable user is assigned the value alice. This group variable is available for demo1.example.com and demo2.example.com with the same value.

- inventory_host_dir

```
[servers]
demo1.example.com
```

- host_vars/demo1.example.com

  ansible_user=devops

- inventory_group_dir

  ```
  [servers]
  demo1.example.com
  demo2.example.com
  ```

- group_vars/servers

  user=alice

You can achieve the same result by also using directories to populate host and group variables. As you can see, the result are the same as the previous example but using more files. In the left column, you see an example of a host variable. The variable ansible_user is assigned the value devops. This host variable is available for demo1.example.com. On the right column, you see an example of a group variable. The variable user is assigned the value alice. This group variable is available for demo1.example.com and demo2.example.com with the same value.

Array Variables

- array.yml

  ```
  ---
  - name: Array demo
    hosts: all
    vars:
      users:
        alice:
          firstname: Alice
          homedir: /users/alice
        bob:
          firstname: Bob
          homedir: /users/bob
  ```

```
        tasks:
          - name: Alice's first name
            ansible.builtin.debug:
                var: users['alice']['firstname']
file name: array.yml
Users are organized in a hierarchical data structure.

Returns 'Alice'
users.alice.firstname
Returns 'Alice'
users['alice']['firstname']
```

An array is a very useful data structure. You can organize the information in a hierarchical data structure. In the example, it's easy to read the list of users: alice and bob. Each element of the list has two properties: `firstname` and `homedir`. You can access the data with dot notation or square brackets. In both cases, you obtain the same result.

array.yml Execution

```
$ ansible-playbook -i inventory array.yml
```

The output includes

- Target host: `demo.example.com`

- Command result: `ok=2`

- Return value:

```
ok: [demo.example.com] => {
    "users['alice']['firstname']": "Alice"
}
```

This output of the execution of `array.yml` is very similar to the previous one. Note the output of "Print Alice's first name: Alice". Ansible accessed the array variable value and showed it in the output message as expected.

Registered Variables

- registeredvariables.yml

```
---
- name: wget installed demo
  hosts: all
  become: true
  tasks:
    - name: wget installed
      ansible.builtin.yum:
        name: wget
        state: present
      register: install_result

    - name: yum printout
      ansible.builtin.debug:
        var: install_result
file name: registeredvariables.yml
```

```
Store the standard output in the variable install_result
that could be printed as well
```

Another very useful data structure is a registered variable. You can save the output of any commands inside a registered variable. This example will be printed on the screen.

registeredvariables.yml Execution

```
$ ansible-playbook -i inventory registeredvariables.yml
```

The output includes

- Target host: demo.example.com

- Command result: ok=3

- Return value:

```
ok: [demo1example.com] => {
    "install_result": {
        "changed": false,
        "failed": false,
        "msg": "Nothing to do",
        "rc": 0,
        "results": []
    }
}
```

This is the output of the execution of `registeredvariables.yml`, as expected. At first, the yum module verifies the presence of the package. If it's missing, it proceeds with the installation. The output of the setup process is stored inside a registered variable that is printed on the screen.

Filters and Templates

You can perform some alterations of variables or configuration files using the Ansible native support for Jinja2 filters and templates. They are parts that extend the functionality of the Ansible control node. Ansible filters manipulate data at a variable level. The most common are

- Assigning default mandatory values

  `{{ variable_name | default(5) }}`

- Making variables optional

  `{{ variable_name | default(omit) }}`

- Assigning a ternary value

  `{{ status | ternary('restart', 'continue') }}`

- Managing data types

  `{{ variable_name | items2dict }}`

- Formatting data to JSON and YAML

  `{{ variable_name | to_json }}`, `{{ variable_name | to_nice_yaml }}`

- Working with regex

```
{{ "ansible" | regex_replace('^.', 'A') }}
```

Ansible templates work similarly by taking advantage of the Jinja2 programming language via the Ansible built-in template module.

Recap

In this section, you explored variable usage inside the Ansible Playbook. You now are aware of the use of tools like the user-defined host, group, and registered variables.

Facts and Magic Variables

In this section, I'll explain what Ansible facts and magic variables are, why you need them, the different types, and how to edit and use them in your day-to-day journey.

Ansible Facts

In Ansible jargon, the system variables related to target hosts are called **facts.** Inside them you can find system information or runtime values, as well as the use of the behavior or the state of the system as configuration on other systems.

They are so powerful because you can obtain a very comprehensive vision of the current host, the operating system, the distribution used, the IP address, the networking configuration, the storage configuration, and more.

Listing All Facts About a Machine Ad-Hoc

```
$ ansible -m setup one.example.com
demo.example.com | SUCCESS => {
  "ansible_facts": {
    "ansible_all_ipv4_addresses": [
      "192.168.43.35",
      "10.0.2.15"
    ],
```

```
"ansible_all_ipv6_addresses": [
  "fe80::a00:27ff:fe71:bd5a"
],
"ansible_apparmor": {
  "status": "disabled"
},
"ansible_architecture": "x86_64",
"ansible_bios_date": "12/01/2006",
"ansible_bios_vendor": "innotek GmbH",
"ansible_bios_version": "VirtualBox",
"ansible_board_asset_tag": "NA",
"ansible_board_name": "VirtualBox",
"ansible_board_serial": "NA",
"ansible_board_vendor": "Oracle Corporation",
"ansible_board_version": "1.2",
"ansible_chassis_asset_tag": "NA",
"ansible_chassis_serial": "NA",
"ansible_chassis_vendor": "Oracle Corporation",
"ansible_chassis_version": "NA",
"ansible_cmdline": {
  "BOOT_IMAGE": "(hd0,msdos1)/vmlinuz-4.18.0-348.el8.x86_64",
  "biosdevname": "0",
  "crashkernel": "auto",
  "net.ifnames": "0",
  "no_timer_check": true,
  "quiet": true,
  "rd.lvm.lv": "rhel_rhel8/swap",
  "resume": "/dev/mapper/rhel_rhel8-swap",
  "rhgb": true,
  "ro": true,
  "root": "/dev/mapper/rhel_rhel8-root"
},
"ansible_date_time": {
  "date": "2022-07-22",
  "day": "22",
```

```
"epoch": "1658504009",
"epoch_int": "1658504009",
"hour": "15",
```

The best way to understand Ansible facts is to list them by yourself using this simple ad-hoc command. You will be surprised by the amount of information you're going to obtain from the host, such as the current hardware configuration, architecture, processor, RAM, available memory, storage configuration, and so on. There is also information about the software configuration, such as operating system, the distribution used, the IP address, the networking configuration, the storage configuration, and more.

Listing All Facts of a Machine Playbook

- facts_printall.yml

```
---
- name: facts_printall
  hosts: all
  tasks:
  - name: Print all facts
    ansible.builtin.debug:
      var: ansible_facts
```

You can access the same amount of data from the Ansible Playbook. In this simple example, you list all Ansible facts for all hosts of the inventory. The expected result will be the same as the previous ad-hoc execution.

facts_printall.yml Execution

```
ansible-playbook -i inventory facts_printall.yml
PLAY [facts_printall] *****************************************
TASK [Gathering Facts] ***************************************
ok: [host1.example.com]
TASK [Print all facts] ***************************************
ok: [host1.example.com] => {
    "ansible_facts": {
        "architecture": "x86_64",
        "bios_date": "10/12/2020",
```

```
        "bios_version": "N22ET66W (1.43 )",
        "br_4332d8483447": {
            "active": false,
            "device": "br-4332d8483447",
            "features": {
                "esp_hw_offload": "off [fixed]",
                "esp_tx_csum_hw_offload": "off [fixed]",
                "fcoe_mtu": "off [fixed]",
```

This is the output of the execution of facts_printall.yml. In this execution, the play is executed against the host1.example.com node. The output is very long, with all the facts obtained automatically by Ansible in the task Gathering Facts. I encourage you to run this code to get confident with Ansible facts.

Referencing a Fact

- facts_printone.yml

```
---
- name: facts_printone
  hosts: all
  tasks:
  - name: Print a fact
    ansible.builtin.debug:
      var: "{{ ansible_facts['architecture'] }}"
```

You can easily interact with facts by specifying the fact name. In this example, you're listing the architecture of the managed nodes (example: architecture: x86_64). Feel free to customize the code to the Ansible facts that better fit your needs.

Magic Variables

Magic variables are internal variables of Ansible used to expose some system status or runtime configurations.

Common Magic Variables

- hostvars
- groups
- group_names
- inventory_hostname
- ansible_version

With the hostvars magic variable, you can access variables defined for any host in the play. It is very useful when you want to access the property of one host from another one. You can combine hostvars with Ansible facts to access a property of other hosts. The groups magic variable lists all the groups in the inventory. You can use groups and hostvars magic variables together to list all the IP addresses of the hosts in a group. group_names is a list of which groups the current host is part of. The Inventory_hostname magic variable contains the name of the host configured in the inventory. The ansible_version magic variable contains the version information about Ansible.

Recap

Ansible facts and magic variables are very useful in your Ansible Playbook especially when you need to execute operations that impact all hosts in the inventory. For example, to generate a custom /etc/hosts file for all the hosts involved in the inventory, you can apply a loop or other statements, which you're going to explore in the next lessons.

Vault

In this section, I am going to talk about how to store secured and encrypted sensitive data (passwords, API keys, usernames, tokens, etc.) using Ansible Vault. Ansible Vault stores variables and files in an encrypted way and lets you use them in Playbooks or roles. The encryption is strong using AES 256 as a cipher to protect your files in the recent versions of Ansible. The ansible-vault command line utility is used to manage Ansible Vault files.

Example of contents of a file encrypted with the ansible-vault tool:

$ANSIBLE_VAULT;1.1;AES256
3939306138313064663135333963626362333636623739636139343962623236616 43
06137333230
3239633330353939363733316661336339396233373337300a3431326236366538356
23030316565
[...]

Creating an Encrypted File

The create parameter of the ansible-vault tool enables the file creation followed by the filename, so the full command for the secret.yml file should be

```
$ ansible-vault create secret.yml
New Vault password: password
Confirm New Vault password: password
```

The command prompts for the vault password to be used two times and then opens a new file using your terminal default editor (Vim, Nano, Emacs, etc.). In this example, the password used is **password** but I strongly encourage you to use one as secure as possible.

You can also store the password in a file (password.txt) and pass it as a parameter using the --vault-password-file= option:

```
$ ansible-vault create --vault-password-file=password.txt secret.yml
```

Viewing an Encrypted File

The view parameter of the ansible-vault tool enables you to read the encrypted file followed by the filename, so the full command for the secret.yml file should be

```
$ ansible-vault view secret.yml
Vault password: password
INFERNO.
I.
Nel mezzo del cammin di nostra vita
mi ritrovai per una selva oscura
ché la diritta via era smarrita.
```

```
Ahi quanto a dir qual era è cosa dura
esta selva selvaggia e aspra e forte
che nel pensier rinova la paura!
Tant'è amara che poco è più morte;
ma per trattar del ben ch'i' vi trovai,
dirò de l'altre cose ch'i' v'ho scorte.
```

Please note that you can use the `ansible-vault view filename` command to view an Ansible Vault-encrypted file without opening it for editing.

Editing an Existing Encrypted File

The `edit` parameter of the `ansible-vault` tool enables the file editing followed by the filename, so the full command for the `secret.yml` file should be

```
$ ansible-vault edit secret.yml
Vault password: password
```

This command allows you to edit an encrypted file. Behind the scenes, the command decrypts the file, makes the changes, and saves the newly encrypted files. All the operations are executed in a securc way.

Encrypting an Existing File

The `encrypt` parameter followed by the filename of the `ansible-vault` tool enables you to encrypt of any clear text (not-encrypted) Ansible Playbook file to Ansible Vault. The full command from `cleartext.yml` to `secret.yml` file should be

```
$ ansible-vault encrypt cleartext.yml --output=secret.yml
New Vault password: password
Confirm New Vault password: password
Encryption successful
```

Please note that if you omit the `--output` option, the original file will be overwritten with the encrypted one.

Decrypting an Existing File

The decrypt parameter followed by the filename of the ansible-vault tool enables you to decrypt any Ansible Vault to a clear text (not-encrypted) Ansible Playbook file. The full command from secret.yml to cleartext.yml file should be

```
$ ansible-vault decrypt secret.yml --output=cleartext.yml
Vault password: password
Decryption successful
```

Please note that if you omit the --output option, the original file will be overwritten with the decrypted one.

Changing the Password of an Encrypted File

The rekey parameter followed by the filename of the ansible-vault tool enables you to change of the password of any Ansible Vault file. The full command for the secret.yml file should be

```
$ ansible-vault rekey secret.yml
Vault password: password1
New Vault password: password
Confirm New Vault password: password
Rekey successful
```

This command also allows you to rekey multiple Ansible Vault files at once. It prompts for the original password and then the new password.

Playbooks and Ansible Vault

```
$ ansible-playbook playbook.yml
TASK [include_vars] ********************************fatal: [localhost]:
FAILED! => {"ansible_facts": {}, "ansible_included_var_files": [], "changed":
false, "message": "Attempting to decrypt but no vault secrets found"}

$ ansible-playbook --vault-id name@prompt playbook.yml
Vault password (default): password

$ ansible-playbook --vault-password-file=vault-password.txt playbook.yml
```

To run a Playbook that accesses files encrypted with Ansible Vault, you need to provide the encryption password to the `ansible-playbook` command. If you do not provide the password, the Playbook will return an error. To provide the Vault password to the Playbook, use the --ask-vault-pass or the `--vault-id` option. For example, to provide the Vault password interactively, use `--vault-id name@prompt` as illustrated for the Vault named "name." Alternatively, you could use a password file.

Recap

In this section, you explored the Ansible Vault security storage to save secrets and confidential information inside Ansible. As you saw, these tools are robust and completely integrated inside the Ansible technology.

Conditional

In this section, I'll explain what Ansible conditional operations are and how you can use them every day in your Ansible Playbook. A conditional statement checks a condition and performs one or a set of tasks accordingly.

Computers have the ability to execute a huge amount of operations and tasks. Sometimes you need to execute one task or a set of tasks only when some conditions are happening. Common use cases involve specific values of a variable, in most cases boolean (`True` or `False`), some environment variables, some running conditions, or some specific version of the operating system in the running node. In Ansible, you express the conditional with the when statement. It's very powerful because it's based on the Jinjia2 tests and filters. You may also specify complex expressions, combined by traditional comparison operators and also by the and, or, and not logical operations. You can use the built-in Ansible tests and filters or expand with a collection or create your own. The code is executed only when the result of the when expression is `True`.

For example, let's imagine an Ansible Playbook that installs a web server on Linux. You need to use YUM/DNF-specific code for RedHat-like systems, APT for Debian-like systems, and ZYPPER for Suse-like systems. Another example is the need to install a different package name or version based on the operating system version, such as version 8 and version 9 of the Red Hat Enterprise Linux.

Basic Conditionals with "when"

- conditional_basic_false.yml

```
---
- name: conditional_basic
  hosts: all
  vars:
    configure_nginx: false
  tasks:
    - name: reload nginx
      ansible.builtin.service:
        name: nginx
        state: reloaded
      when: configure_nginx
```

This is the basic example of the usage of the when statement in your Ansible playbook. The task reload nginx is executed only when the configure_nginx boolean variable is set to true. We expect this task to be skipped. Let's see the output of the executed code.

The execution output includes

- Target host: demo1.example.com

- Command result: skipping=1

- Return value:

```
TASK [reload nginx]
skipping: [demo1.example.com]
```

This is the output of the execution of conditional_basic_false.yml. In this execution, the play is executed against the demo1.example.com node. The output is highlighted with green and blue colors. As you can see, the task of the task reload nginx is read by Ansible but skipped based on the conditional statement.

- conditional_basic_true.yml

```
---
- name: conditional_basic
  hosts: all
  vars:
    configure_nginx: true
  tasks:
    - name: reload nginx
      ansible.builtin.service:
        name: nginx
        state: reloaded
      when: configure_nginx
```

This is the same basic example of the usage of the when statement in your Ansible Playbook but you changed the variable value from false to true. The task reload nginx is now going to be executed because the configure_nginx boolean variable is set to true. Let's see the output of this code execution.

The execution output includes

- Target host: demo1.example.com

- Command result: ok=2

- Return value:

```
TASK [reload nginx]
ok: [demo1.example.com
```

This is the output of the execution of conditional_basic_true.yml. In this execution, the play is executed against the demo1.example.com node. The output is highlighted in green. As you can see, the task of the task reload nginx is read by Ansible and executed successfully in the conditional statement.

Conditionals Based on ansible_facts

- conditional_facts.yml

```
---
- name: conditional_facts
  hosts: all
  tasks:
  - name: Shut down Debian-like systems
    ansible.builtin.command: /sbin/shutdown -t now
    when: ansible_facts['os_family'] == "Debian"
```

It is very useful to combine conditional and facts. You can adapt the execution of your code based on variable values, runtime conditions, the value of the IP address, the version of the operating system, some storage or file system object status, and so on. In this example, suppose you want to shut down only the Debian-like target system, so Debian and Ubuntu managed hosts.

The execution output includes

- Target host: demo1.example.com

- Command result: skipped=1

- Return value:

  ```
  TASK [Shut down Debian-like systems]
  skipping: [demo1.example.com]
  ```

As you can see, the status of the task Shut down Debian-like systems on the target demo1.example.com is skipped. This means that the system demo1.example.com isn't using a Debian-like Linux operating system.

Recap

Conditionals are very important because they enable you to create Ansible Playbooks that respond to some events, conditions, or Ansible facts. This statement is the foundation of the smart Ansible Playbook.

Loop

In this section, I'll explain what Ansible loop operations are and how you can use them every day in your Ansible Playbook. Loops automate repetitive tasks.

Computers are great for the fast execution of a block of code of tasks. According to Moore's Law, every two years the number of transistors doubles in a dense integrated circuit. Computers are faster than any human on the planet and they make no mistakes. In computers, programming language loops are also called *iterations*. Ansible includes several statements for iteration: the `loop` statement and the `with_items` statements. The `with` statement relies on plugins.

- `loop_simple.yml`

```
---
- name: Check services
  hosts: all
  tasks:
  - name: httpd and mariadb are running
    ansible.builtin.service:
      name: "{{ item }}"
      state: started
    loop:
      - httpd
      - mariadb
```

This example checks that two services (`httpd` and `mariadb`) are in the "started" state. Every service name is listed directly as a list element under the `loop` statement. Please note the usage of the variable `item` that iterates the current values in each iteration. Here `item` is going to be expanded for each element of the list (in this case, `httpd` and `mariadb`).

- `loop_hash_or_dict.yml`

```
---
- name: users and group example
  hosts: all
  tasks:
  - name: add users to groups
```

```
    ansible.builtin.user:
      name: "{{ item.name }}"
      state: present
      groups: "{{ item.group }}"
  loop:
    - name: alice
      group: wheel
    - name: bob
      group: root
```

Some use cases require more complex iteration variable types such as hashes or dictionaries. As always, Ansible relies heavily on Python data types. This is an example of a dictionary with two keys: name and group for each element of the list. You can access the current item loop variable using a dot. Specifically, name can be retrieved with the item.name and group with item.group variables, respectively.

with_* Statement

- with_items

Like loop for simple lists, a list of strings, or a list of hashes/dictionaries. Faster to list if lists of lists are provided

- with_file

This keyword requires a list of control node file names. The loop variable item holds the content of the file

- with_sequence

Requires parameters to generate a list of values based on a numeric sequence. From 0 to 10, for example.

loop_with_items.yml

```
---
- name: Example with_items
  hosts: all
```

```
vars:
  data:
    - alice
    - bob
tasks:
- name: Print values of data
  ansible.builtin.debug:
    msg: "{{ item }}"
  with_items: "{{ data }}"
```

In the `loop_with_items.yml` Ansible Playbook, the variable `data` is a list of strings. The task `Print values of data` uses `with_items` to iterate item by item and print on the screen.

Recap

Loops statements are very useful to automate repetitive tasks. Loops are the foundation of a successful Ansible Playbook.

Handler

In this section, I'll explain what an Ansible Handler statement is and how you can use it every day in your Ansible Playbook.

`Handlers run operations on change`

Handlers are very important for idempotency. They allow you to execute some steps only if necessary and to save computer cycles when there is no need for them to be executed.

rollingupdate.yml

```
---
- name: Rolling update
  hosts: all
  become: true
```

```
tasks:
  - name: latest apache httpd package is installed
    ansible.builtin.yum:
      name: httpd
      state: latest
    notify: restart apache

handlers:
  - name: restart apache
    ansible.builtin.service:
      name: httpd
      state: restarted
```

The `rollingupdate.yml` file is composed by one task and one handler. The handler code is executed only if necessary. Please note the `notify` statement; it mentions the name of the handler to run. This Playbook checks the version of the Apache http web server on all hosts. If an update is available, the yum module provides the upgrade process and restarts the daemon at the end. If an upgrade is not necessary, the handler code is not necessary. A more complex Playbook can have multiple handlers and you can reference them by name.

Role

In this section, I'll explain what Ansible's role is in code reuse and how you can use it every day in your Ansible Playbook. The Ansible role enables code reuse in Ansible.

Roles are like functions in the traditional programming world. An Ansible role enables code reuse and sharing in a public directory called Ansible Galaxy (`https://galaxy.ansible.com/`). Creators from all over the world contribute code in the Ansible Galaxy directory. The usage of Ansible roles dramatically speeds up any Ansible Playbook development, enabling access to a lot of high-quality resources. Another amazing public resource is the Linux System Roles: A collection of Ansible roles and modules at `https://linux-system-roles.github.io/at`.

Role Tree Directories

This is a directory tree example of the `role.example` Ansible role:

```
role.example/
|-- defaults
|   `-- main.yml
|-- files
|-- handlers
|   `-- main.yml
|-- meta
|   `-- main.yml
|-- README.md
|-- tasks
|   `-- main.yml
|-- templates
|-- tests
|   |-- inventory
|   `-- test.yml
`-- vars
    `-- main.yml
```

Please note that not every role will have all of these directories but it's good to know the scope and how to take advantage of them in your coding.

Directory description:

- `defaults`

In the `main.yml` file you can define the default value for each variable user in the role. These variables are intended to be overwritten in your Playbook when you execute the role.

- `files`

In the `files` directory, you store all the static files present inside by role tasks.

- `handlers`

Every handler is supposed to be defined in the `main.yml` file under this directory.

- `meta`

CHAPTER 1   ANSIBLE FOR BEGINNERS WITH EXAMPLES

This is the most descriptive part of the Ansible role, and the `main.yml` file includes information about the creator, the files license, the tested platforms, and optionally the Ansible role dependencies.

- `tasks`

This is the heart of your automation and effectively contains all the Ansible tasks to be executed.

- `templates`

All Jinja2 templates of the role are under this directory.

- `tests`

Any code to test the Ansible role was originally stored under this directory. Nowadays it's substituted by the Ansible Molecule project (`https://molecule.readthedocs.io/en/latest/`).

- `vars`

The `main.yml` file in this directory represents the Ansible role's internal variables. Often these variables are used for internal purposes within the role. These variables have high precedence and are not intended to be changed when used in a Playbook.

Using Ansible Roles in a Playbook

- `./role_simple.yml`

```
---

- name: role example
  hosts: all
  roles:
     - role1
     - role2
file name: role_simple.yml
Apply the "role1" and "role2" to the "all" managed hosts
```

- ./role_vars.yml

```
---
- name: role example
  hosts: all
  roles:
    - role: role1
    - role: role2
      var1: value
      var2: value
  file name: role_vars.yml
  Apply the "role1" and "role2" to the "all" managed hosts

  "role2" has two variables parameters
```

Order of Execution

- ./role_vars.yml

```
---
- name: order of execution example
  hosts: all
  pre_tasks:
    - debug:
        msg: 'pre-task'
      notify: my handler
  roles:
    - role1
  tasks:
    - debug:
        msg: 'first task'
      notify: my handler
  post_tasks:
    - debug:
        msg: 'post-task'
      notify: my handler
```

```
handlers:
  - name: my handler
    debug:
      msg: Running my handler
```

For each play in a Playbook, tasks execute as ordered in the tasks list. After all tasks execute, any notified handlers are executed. When a role is added to a play, role tasks are added to the beginning of the tasks list. If a second role is included in a play, its tasks list is added after the first role. Role handlers are added to plays in the same manner that role tasks are added to plays. Each play defines a handler's list. Role handlers are added to the handlers list first, followed by any handlers defined in the handlers section of the play. In certain scenarios, it may be necessary to execute some play tasks before the roles. To support such scenarios, plays can be configured with a `pre_tasks` section. Any task listed in this section executes before any roles are executed. If any of these tasks notify a handler, those handler tasks execute before the roles or normal tasks. Plays also support a `post_tasks` keyword. These tasks execute after the play's normal tasks, and any handlers they notify are run.

Ansible Galaxy

- https://galaxy.ansible.com/

Installing Roles from Ansible Galaxy Manually

```
$ ansible-galaxy install geerlingguy.redis -p roles/
```

Installing Roles from Ansible Galaxy requirements.yml

The `requirements.yml` file allows you to specify all the Ansible roles you need in a row. For example, the following file allows you to install the `geerlingguy.redis` Ansible role version `1.5.0`. If you omit the version, the latest release is used.

Best practices recommend storing the `requirements.yml` file under the roles directory of your Ansible project.

- roles/requirements.yml

```
- src: geerlingguy.redis
  version: "1.5.0"
```

It's super easy to consume the `requirements.yml` files using the `ansible-galaxy` tool.

```
$ ansible-galaxy install -r roles/requirements.yml  -p roles
```

The option `-r` allows you to recursively install all the necessary dependencies of your Ansible role. The option `-p` as usual specifies the target directory in your filesystem.

Collection

An Ansible Collection is a distribution format for shipping some Ansible resources. It is usually specific for a single use case and contains all the relevant Ansible resources that distribute playbooks, roles, modules, and plugins. For users, the Ansible Collection is easy to download and share via the Ansible Galaxy directory. For developers, the Ansible Collection is easy to upload and share via Ansible Galaxy. Plus, an Ansible Collection has a defined standard directory structure and format.

Refer to the "Installation of the Additional Collection" section in Chapter 2 for some code samples about how to install the community.vmware Ansible Collection.

Ansible Plugins

Plugins extend the functionality of Ansible and unlock many applications. For example, the lookup plugins enable you to extend Jinja2 to access data from outside sources within your playbooks, and they execute and are evaluated on the Ansible control node. Famous use cases are for reading from Windows INI style files (ini), reading from CSV files (csvfile), listening files matching shell expressions (fileglob), reading lines from stdout (lines), generating a random password (password), reading from a Unix pipe (pipe), and returning content from a URL via HTTP or HTTPS (url).

The full list of plugin types includes action, cache, callback, connection, filter, inventory, lookup, test, and vars.

Please refer to the official "Ansible Working with Plugins" guide at `https://docs.ansible.com/ansible/latest/plugins/plugins.html` for more details.

Key Takeaways

Whether a beginner or an experienced Ansible user, you now have more familiarity with the Ansible code language, architecture, and terminology. You explored concepts like ad-hoc commands, inventories, Playbooks, variables, facts and magic variables, vaults, conditionals, loops, handlers, roles, and Collections.

In the next chapter, you are going to install an Ansible control node on the most used operating systems. The following chapter is completely focused on VMware automation with Ansible.

CHAPTER 2

Installing Ansible

It is simple to install most common and modern operating system nowadays. The main requirements for Ansible are only the Python interpreter and some Python libraries to read and format YAML documents and to interact with SSH for Linux/macOS target hosts and WinRM for Windows target hosts. All of this is handled by the operating system package manager, so you don't need to worry about it. Ansible is already included in most recent Linux distributions out of the box. Most of the time, this doesn't require additional repositories or complex commands. You can install Ansible simply by using the distribution package manager or the Python Package Manager (PIP). After the installation, you start your journey simply typing "ansible" in your favorite terminal. Ansible is able to handle every workload from a simple "ping" module to testing the connection to the target node to a complex automation workflow (also called an Ansible Playbook).

Ansible Community vs. ansible-core Packages

At the moment, there are two ways to install Ansible in your system: the `ansible-core` package and the Ansible community package . These packages always confuse early adopters as well as some long-time users (after Ansible version 2.9). These two packages respond to the needs of different use cases. The Ansible community package is maintained by the Ansible community, while `ansible-core` is maintained by the Ansible Engineering Team. The Ansible community package offers the functionality of `ansible-core` plus 85+ collections containing thousands of modules and plugins. The Ansible Engineering Team focuses on stability and reliability, while the Ansible community strives to provide the latest features and functionality to a broader audience. If you need the full Ansible experience and the latest and greatest features, the Ansible community package is the way to go. However, if you need only the Ansible stable and reliable platform, `ansible-core` is the better choice.

© Luca Berton 2023
L. Berton, *Ansible for VMware by Examples*, https://doi.org/10.1007/978-1-4842-8879-5_2

Before 2021 and until Ansible version 2.9, the Ansible Engineering Team released only one package with the Ansible platform and all the additional collection codes in one package called `ansible`, similar to the Ansible community package. The main drawback of this release approach was that the size of the package was too much (hundreds of MB of storage space) for content that was used rarely by customers. Another big drawback was that the bug fixes required waiting for the next release cycle. By 2021, starting with version 2.10, Ansible Engineering Team decided to focus on the `ansible-core` package. The `ansible-core` package contains the Ansible platform, the runtime tools, and the `ansible.builtin` modules and plugins collection. A crazy note: The 2.10 version of the `ansible-core` package was initially called `ansible-base`. The advantage of this approach is the smallest possible storage platform footprint and a release cycle based only on the Ansible technology. The Ansible community package is a convenient release of the `ansible-core` platform plus all the additional modules and plugins of other available Ansible collections. The most famous and most used collections are `community.general` for UNIX and POSIX utilities, `community.windows` for Windows target hosts, `amazon.aws` for Amazon Web Services, `community.azure` for Azure, `kubernetes.core` for Kubernetes, and `community.postgresql` for PostgreSQL. In summary, Ansible distributes two deliverables: the latest and greatest features in the Ansible community package and a minimalist platform called `ansible-core`. Generally speaking, if you're in a production environment, you should prefer the `ansible-core` package plus only the needed collections. If you are a developer, you might prefer the Ansible community package with all the tools and additional collections. Apart from this general advice, you can choose the Ansible package that fits your need. These packages allow you more flexibility and storage savings, especially for production virtual machines and containers use cases.

At the writing of this book, the Ansible Engineering Team released version 2.14.0 of the `ansible-core` package, and the Ansible Community Team released version `6.1.0` of The Ansible community package (July 2022).

You can check your currently running Ansible release using the `ansible` command with the `--version` parameter. The first line of the output should show you the exact running version. The version below uses the release number 2, major 13, and minor 1:

```
ansible [core 2.13.1]
```

You can get more details on the current releases and maintenance plans on the Ansible official website.

ansible-core

The `ansible-core` package is for Ansible expert users or production systems. It contains only the Ansible platform technology and enables you to install the additional collections. This is the main building block of the Ansible architecture. The `ansible-core` package includes the Ansible platform for developing the Ansible Playbooks such as conditionals and blocks, and it includes a loop and other Ansible imperatives plus an extensive architectural framework to enable Ansible collections and all the command-line tools for interacting with automation (`ansible-playbook`, `ansible-doc`, etc.) The release cycle is approximately twice per year by the Ansible Engineering Team.

The Ansible Community Package

The most complete Ansible experience is guaranteed by the Ansible community package, which contains thousands of modules and plugins and the `ansible-core` platform. The Ansible community package includes the `ansible-core` Ansible platform and 85+ collections containing thousands of modules and plugins. It requires the `ansible-core` package to be installed on the system. The release cycle is approximately twice per year by the Ansible community, following the `ansible-core` release plan.

Additional Collections Installation

Both Ansible platforms can be extended using additional Ansible collection resources. Read more about the current Collection Index on the Ansible official website.

The ansible command-line tool, ansible-galaxy, is designed to easily download and maintain any collection in your system. Suppose you want to download the community.vmware collection via the `ansible-galaxy` command. You can specify the collection name straightaway or via a `requirements.yml` file.

Installing the community.vmware Collection via the ansible-galaxy Command

Let's see how to install the community.vmware collection via the `ansible-galaxy` command:

```
$ ansible-galaxy collection install community.vmware
```

Installing the community.vmware Collection via the requirements.yml File

You can automate the installation of the community.vmware collection using the requirements.yml file for the ansible-galaxy command. The Ansible best practices recommend storing the requirements.yml file under the collections directory of your Ansible project: collections/requirements.yml.

```
---
collections:
  - name: community.vmware
    source: https://galaxy.ansible.com

    – command execution
```

```
$ ansible-galaxy install -r collections/requirements.yml
```

Verifying the Currently Installed Version of community.vmware

After a successful installation, you can verify the currently installed version of the community.vmware using the command line:

```
$ ansible-galaxy collection list community.vmware
```

The command may return multiple results if they apply, with the relevant file system path and version(s). If no result is returned, it means that no versions of the Ansible collection are currently installed in the system right now.

Links

- Ansible Core official documentation, https://docs.ansible.com/ansible-core/devel/index.html

- ansible-core package, https://pypi.org/project/ansible-core/

- Ansible community package, https://pypi.org/project/ansible/

Ansible Installation for RedHat Enterprise Linux (RHEL) 8

You can install the latest release of Ansible in Red Hat Enterprise Linux version 8 using the Ansible Engine Software Collections (RHSCL) using the YUM/DNF distribution tools.

The easier way to install and maintain Ansible inside Red Hat Enterprise Linux version 8 is by using the DNF package manager (previously on RHEL known as YUM). The repository that contains Ansible 2.9 is called the Ansible Engine Software Collection, `ansible-2.9-for-rhel-8-x86_64-rpms`. The main advantage of using RHSCL is that you don't need any external repository such as EPEL for this content. Software collections (RHSCL) are fully supported by Red Hat and included in your subscription plan.

Please note that `ansible-core` is supported since RedHat Enterprise Linux (RHEL) version 8.6 and version 9.0.

- ansible-core for RHEL 8.6 and 9.0 AppStream repository, `www.redhat.com/en/blog/updates-using-ansible-rhel-86-and-90`

- Activate the EPEL (Extra Packages for Enterprise Linux) repository, `https://docs.fedoraproject.org/en-US/epel/`

Code

The following code installs the latest version of Ansible 2.9 in your RedHat Enterprise Linux (RHEL) 8.

- Install Ansible RHEL8

Please note you need `root` privileges to execute the following commands. First, you need to enable the RHSCL using the `subscription-manager` tool:

```
# subscription-manager repos --enable ansible-2.9-for-rhel-8-x86_64-rpms
```

Then you can perform the installation of the `ansible` package using the YUM or DNF tool:

```
# yum install ansible
```

This command installs the Ansible package as well as all the needed dependencies `python3-babel`, `python3-cffi`, `python3-cryptography`, `python3-jinja2`, `python3-markupsafe`, `python3-pycparser`, `python3-pytz`, `python3-pyyaml`, `sshpass`, and weak dependency `python3-jmespath`.

- Verification

You can verify the successful installation of Ansible using the `ansible --version` command in any terminal. At the time of writing this book, it's available in version 2.9.27 on Python 3.6.8 (July 2022).

Ansible Installation for Ubuntu 22.04 LTS

You can perform the installation of the latest release of Ansible in Ubuntu 22.04 LTS via the **universe** and **PPA** repositories using the distribution package manager (APT). The first method to install Ansible is by using the universe repository, the default that you get after installation. The main advantage of using the universe repository is that you don't require any external repository. The second method to install Ansible is by using the Personal Package Archives (PPA) repository. Please bear in mind that adding repositories mean different quality assurances.

Code

You can install the Ansible package in Ubuntu 22.04 LTS with the `universe` and `ansible/ansible` PPA repositories.

universe

- Install-Ubuntu-Universe.sh

Please note you need `root` privileges to execute the following commands or use `sudo` before the following commands. First, you may need to update the package manager metadata cache using the `apt` tool:

```
# apt update
```

Then you can install the `ansible` package using the `apt` or `apt-get` tool:

```
# apt install ansible
```

This command installs the ansible package as well as all the needed dependencies: `ieee-data`, `python3-argcomplete`, `python3-dnspython`, `python3-jmespath`, `python3-kerberos`, `python3-libcloud`, `python3-lockfile`, `python3-netaddr`, `python3-ntlm-auth`, `python3-packaging`, `python3-pycryptodome`, `python3-`

requests-kerberos, python3-requests-ntlm, python3-requests-toolbelt, python3-selinux, python3-simplejson, python3-winrm, and python3-xmltodict.

- Verification

You can verify the successful installation of Ansible using the ansible --version command in any terminal. At the time of writing this book, it's available in ansible-core version 2.10.8 on Python 3.10.4 (July 2022).

PPA

- Install-Ubuntu-PPA.sh

If you prefer to install ansible-core using the ansible/ansible PPA repository, you must first enable it using this command:

```
# add-apt-repository --yes --update ppa:ansible/ansible
```

Please verify that the Ansible package isn't installed or remove it using the command (expect a failure otherwise):

```
# apt remove ansible
```

Finally, you can use the ansible-core command:

```
# apt install ansible-core
```

- Verification

You can verify the successful installation of Ansible using the ansible --version command in any terminal. At the time of writing this book, it's available in ansible-core version 2.12.4 on Python 3.10.4 (July 2022).

Ansible Installation for Fedora 36

You can install and maintain Ansible in Fedora 36 using the AppStream repository for your DNF package manager. The easier way is using DNF and the AppStream repository that comes out of the box with Fedora Linux.

Code

Install Ansible in Fedora version 36 via the AppStream system repository using the `ansible-core` or Ansible community packages.

Please note you need `root` privileges to execute the following commands. You can install the latest release of the Ansible community release using the DNF tool:

- install-Ansible-Fedora.sh

```
# dnf install ansible
```

This command installs the Ansible package as well as all the needed dependencies (`ansible-core`, `libsodium`, `python3-bcrypt`, `python3-jmespath`, `python3-ntlm-auth`, `python3-packaging`, `python3-pynacl`, `python3-pyparsing`, `python3-requests_ntlm`, `python3-resolvelib`, `python3-xmltodict`) and weak dependencies (`python3-paramiko`, `python3-pyasn1`, `python3-winrm`).

- Verification

You can verify the successful installation of Ansible using the `ansible --version` command in any terminal. At the time of writing this book, it's available in `ansible-core` version 2.12.5 on Python 3.10.4 (July 2022).

Ansible Installation for CentOS 9 Stream

You can install and maintain Ansible in CentOS 9 Stream using the AppStream repository or the EPEL Next (Extra Packages for Enterprise Linux) repository for your YUM/DNF package manager. The easier way is by using DNF and the AppStream repository that comes out of the box with CentOS Linux.

- ansible-core package in the system AppStream repository

The easier way to install and maintain Ansible inside CentOS Stream version 9 is using the system AppStream repository.

- Use EPEL Next additional packages for CentOS Stream

Another way is to use the additional EPEL Next repository. This repository contains enterprise-quality packages for CentOS Stream, similar to EPEL packages but targeting RHEL, CentOS, Scientific Linux, and Oracle Linux.

Links

- CentOS Stream download, `www.centos.org/centos-stream/`

- EPEL 9 is now available, `https://communityblog.fedoraproject.org/epel-9-is-now-available/`

- Introducing CentOS Stream 9, `https://blog.centos.org/2021/12/introducing-centos-stream-9/`,

- Install EPEL (Extra Packages for Enterprise Linux), `https://docs.fedoraproject.org/en-US/epel/`

Code

To install the latest release of Ansible Core in CentOS Stream version 9 via the AppStream system repository, please note you need `root` privileges to execute the following commands. You can install the `ansible-core` package using the yum or DNF tool:

- Install-Ansible-CentOS-Stream9.sh

```
# dnf install ansible-core
```

This command installs the Ansible package as well as all the needed dependencies: `emacs-filesystem`, `git`, `git-core`, `git-core-doc`, `perl-Error`, `perl-Git`, `python3-babel`, `python3-cffi`, `python3-cryptography`, `python3-jinja2`, `python3-markupsafe`, `python3-pycparser`, `python3-pytz`, `python3-pyyaml`, and `sshpass`.

- Verification

You can verify the successful installation of Ansible using the `ansible --version` command in any terminal. At the time of writing this book, it's available in `ansible-core` version 2.12.0 on Python 3.9.8 (July 2022).

Ansible Installation on Windows

You can install and maintain Ansible inside Windows via the WSL (Windows Subsystem for Linux) and Ubuntu 20.04 LTS image. WSL is available since Microsoft Windows 10 version 2004 or build 19041 and Windows 11 too.

Officially, Microsoft Windows is **NOT** a supported operating system for the Ansible Control node, but the Ansible Community Team is working hard to eliminate barriers to native Windows controllers. The reason behind this is that there is a lot of POSIX-specific code deeply baked into most of Ansible that prevents it from working on native Windows. Windows doesn't have the `fork()` `syscall` implementation. Ansible Controller Worker model since version 2.11 uses a lot of the POSIX fork() syscall. At the moment, there are two possible workarounds:

- Cygwin

Cygwin enables POSIX compatibility but sometimes the execution just breaks and it's difficult to troubleshoot, so it's not a reliable solution.

- Windows Subsystem for Linux

The best alternative at the moment is to use Windows Subsystem for Linux (WSL). Run WSL version 2 if Windows 10 is later than build 2004 or Windows 11. Ansible works great on WSL version 1 and WSL version 2.

For systems that don't support the nested virtualization technology or a virtualized environment to use the WSL version 2, you must force the WSL version 1 using the `wsl --set-default-version 1` command.

Links

More technical information:

- WSL (Windows Subsystem for Linux), `https://docs.microsoft.com/en-us/windows/wsl/compare-versions`

- Ansible on Windows FAQ, `https://docs.ansible.com/ansible/latest/user_guide/windows_faq.html`

- WSL on Windows 11, `https://arstechnica.com/gadgets/2021/10/the-best-part-of-windows-11-is-a-revamped-windows-subsystem-for-linux/`

Code

To install the latest version of Ansible on Windows using Microsoft WSL, you can activate it by executing PowerShell as a user with administrator rights.

- install_wsl.ps1

```
wsl --install
```

This command takes care of the installation process of all the necessary Microsoft WSL components: Virtual Machine Platform, Windows Subsystem for Linux, WSL Kernel, GUI App Support, and the Ubuntu image. The changes require a system reboot. After a few minutes, you will be able to set up the WSL login credentials (Linux username and password) and proceed with the installation like a real Ubuntu Linux machine.

```
# apt-get install ansible
```

The apt package manager takes care of all the necessary package dependencies from the ubuntu repository: `ieee-data`, `python3-argcomplete`, `python3-crypto`, `python3-dnspython`, `python3-jmespath`, `python3-kerberos`, `python3-libcloud`, `python3-lockfile`, `python3-netaddr`, `python3-ntlm-auth`, `python3-requests-kerberos`, `python3-requests-ntlm`, `python3-selinux`, and `python3-winrm python3-xmltodict`.

- Verification

You can verify the successful installation of Ansible using the `ansible --version` command in any terminal. At the time of writing this book, it's available in `ansible` version 2.9.6 on Python 3.8.2 (July 2022). I suggest evaluating the installation of the latest release of Ansible via PIP in this system.

Ansible Installation for macOS

The easier way to install and maintain Ansible inside macOS is to use the Homebrew package manager from `https://brew.sh/`. The main advantage of using `brew` is that it takes care of all the necessary dependencies, and it also manages the upgrade process. An alternative is to use Python PIP but you need to download the relevant software packages. PIP could be a solution for a developer who always has the latest up-to-date release.

Code

First, verify that the Homebrew package manager is successfully installed on your system or refer to the installation process on the official website (one command line to copy and paste). This step usually requires you to open a terminal on your macOS and type the installation command. When Homebrew is successfully installed, you can proceed with installing `ansible` in your system.

- Install the latest release.

```
$ brew install ansible
```

This command installs the `ansible` package as well as all the needed package dependencies: `openssl` and `sqlite`.

- Verification

You can verify the successful installation of Ansible using the `ansible --version` command in any terminal. At the time of writing this book, it's available in `ansible-core` version 2.13.1 on Python 3.10.5 (July 2022).

Ansible Installation for SUSE SLES (Linux Enterprise Server) 15 SP3

You can install and maintain the Ansible latest version in SUSE Linux Enterprise Server (SLES) version 15 SP3 using the **SUSE Package Hub** repository for the Zypper package manager tool.

Links

- SUSE Package Hub: Community maintained packages for SUSE Linux Enterprise Server/Desktop, `https://packagehub.suse.com/`

- How to register SLES using the SUSEConnect command line tool, `www.suse.com/support/kb/doc/?id=000018564`

- SUSE Package Hub repositories for SUSE Linux Enterprise Server, `www.suse.com/support/kb/doc/?id=000018789`

Code

You can install the latest version of ansible in SUSE Linux Enterprise Server 15 SP3 using the SUSE Package Hub repository. Please adapt the code to your distribution version.

Please note you need root privileges to execute the following commands.

- Install-Ansible-SLES-15-SP3.sh

```
# SUSEConnect -p PackageHub/15.3/x86_64
```

The first line activates the SUSE Package Hub repository and the second installs ansible in your system using the Zypper package manager.

```
# zypper install ansible
```

This command installs the ansible package as well as all the needed dependencies: libsodium23, python3-Babel, python3-Jinja2, python3-MarkupSafe, python3-PyNaCl, python3-PyYAML, python3-appdirs, python3-asn1crypto, python3-bcrypt, python3-cffi, python3-cryptography, python3-jmespath, python3-packaging, python3-paramiko, python3-passlib, python3-ply, python3-pyasn1, python3-pycparser, python3-pycryptodome, python3-pyparsing, python3-pytz, python3-setuptools, python3-simplejson, and python3-six.

- Verification

You can verify the successful installation of Ansible using the ansible --version command in any terminal. At the time of writing this book, it's available in ansible version 2.9.6 on Python 3.6.13 (July 2022). I suggest evaluating the installation of the latest release of Ansible via PIP in this system.

Ansible Installation with PIP

Performing the installation of Ansible using PIP ensures that you always fetch the latest release of the ansible-core or the Ansible community packages. PIP is the Python package manager, and it will take care of all of the processes and manage the necessary dependencies. It takes care of the download and installation process of packages directly from the official PyPI website as well as all the necessary dependencies. PIP is designed to be OS-independent so it's available in a large variety of modern operating systems. It could be a great solution for developers who always want the latest up-to-date release.

The alternative approach is to use the OS-specific package manager, such as Linux YUM, DNF, APT, Zypper, and macOS Homebrew. This second approach puts more emphasis on stability so the latest release may not available yet. If you need the latest release of Ansible, I suggest you use PIP.

Code

You can proceed with the installation of the latest version of Ansible with PIP, the Python package manager.

code PIP

You can install the software for just the current user or system-wide. First, verify that PIP is successfully installed on your system. Usually, you need to install it with your distribution package manager such as yum, DNF, apt, or Zypper.

Please adjust python to python3, and python3.9 as needed.

- Install-pip-user.sh

```
$ python -m pip install --upgrade -user pip
$ python -m pip install --user ansible
```

- Install-pip-global.sh

Installing software system-wide requires root permission privileges.

```
# python -m pip install --upgrade pip
# python -m pip install ansible
```

- Verification

You can verify the successful installation of Ansible using the ansible --version command in any terminal. At the time of writing this book, it's available in ansible-core version 2.13.1 on Python 3.9.2 (July 2022).

Ansible Installation for RedHat Enterprise Linux 9

The latest release of Ansible Core (ansible-core package) for RHEL 9 is inside the system AppStream repository for the DNF package manager.

- ansible-core is included in the RHEL 9 AppStream repository

No additional repositories (such as Ansible Engine or EPEL) like previous versions are necessary for basic automation. However, if you need additional support you should buy the Red Hat Ansible Automation Platform additional subscription.

Links

- Ansible Core package included in the RHEL AppStream, `https://access.redhat.com/articles/6325611`

- Using Ansible in RHEL 9, `https://access.redhat.com/articles/6393321`

Demo

Perform the installation of the latest Ansible-Core in RHEL 9 using the DNF Package Manager.

- Install-Ansible-RHEL9.sh

```
# dnf install ansible-core
```

- Verification

You can verify the successful installation of Ansible using the `ansible --version` command in any terminal. At the time of writing this book, it's available in `ansible-core` version 2.12.2 on Python 3.9.10 (July 2022).

Ansible Installation for Amazon Linux 2 (AWS EC2)

You can install and maintain Ansible in Amazon Linux 2 using the Amazon Extras Library, amazon-linux-extras, or the EPEL additional repositories.

- `ansible2` topic in Extras Library repository

- `ansible` in EPEL

Ansible is included in the Extras Library included in Amazon Linux 2 repository using the `amazon-linux-extras` command. Another option is to install and maintain Ansible inside Amazon Linux 2 using the EPEL additional repository.

Links

- Amazon Linux 2, `https://aws.amazon.com/it/amazon-linux-2/`

- Enable the EPEL repository in Amazon Linux2, `https://aws.amazon.com/it/premiumsupport/knowledge-center/ec2-enable-epel/`

- Extras library (Amazon Linux 2), `https://docs.aws.amazon.com/AWSEC2/latest/UserGuide/amazon-linux-ami-basics.html#extras-library`

- Extra Packages for Enterprise Linux (EPEL), `https://docs.fedoraproject.org/en-US/epel/`

Code

You can install Ansible in Amazon Linux (EC2) 2 using the Amazon Extras Library or the EPEL repositories for the YUM package manager. Let's start with the Amazon Extras Library option.

Please note you need `root` privileges to execute the following commands.

- Install-Ansible-Amazon Linux2-Amazon Extras Library.sh

```
# sudo amazon-linux-extras install ansible2 -y
```

- Verification

You can verify the successful installation of Ansible using the `ansible --version` command in any terminal. At the time of writing this book, it's available in `ansible` version 2.9.23 on Python 2.7.18 (July 2022). You might consider installing the latest `ansible-core` release via PIP in this system.

- EPEL

You can install Ansible in Amazon Linux (EC2) 2 using the EPEL repositories option for the YUM package manager. Please note you need `root` privileges to execute the following commands or use `sudo` command.

- Install-Ansible-Amazon Linux2-EPEL.sh

```
# amazon-linux-extras install epel -y
# yum-config-manager --enable epel
# yum --enablerepo epel install ansible
```

- Verification

You can verify the successful installation of Ansible using the `ansible --version` command in any terminal. At the time of writing this book, it's available in `ansible-core` version 2.9.25 on Python 2.7.18 (July 2022). You might consider installing the latest `ansible-core` release via PIP in this system.

Ansible Installation for Debian 11

You can install and maintain the latest version of Ansible in Debian using APT and the `main` default repository. Ansible is included in the default `main` repository so you can install it simply with your usual package manager, apt. You can expect the latest version of Ansible in the `main` repository.

Code

You can install Ansible in Debian 11 using the apt package manager and the `main` default repository.

- Install-ansible-debian.sh

Please note you need `root` privileges to execute the following commands or use `sudo` before the following commands.

First, you may need to update the package manage metadata cache using the apt tool:

```
# apt update
```

Then you can install the `ansible` package using the `apt` or `apt-get` tool:

```
# apt install ansible
```

This command installs the ansible package as well as all the needed dependencies: `ieee-data`, `python3-argcomplete`, `python3-dnspython`, `python3-jmespath`, `python3-kerberos`, `python3-libcloud`, `python3-lockfile`, `python3-netaddr`, `python3-ntlm-auth`, `python3-packaging`, `python3-pycryptodome`, `python3-requests-kerberos`, `python3-requests-ntlm`, `python3-requests-toolbelt`, `python3-selinux`, `python3-simplejson`, `python3-winrm`, and `python3-xmltodict`.

- Verification

You can verify the successful installation of Ansible using the `ansible --version` command in any terminal. At the time of writing this book, it's available in `ansible` version 2.10.8 on Python 2.9.2 (July 2022). You might consider installing the latest `ansible-core` release via PIP in this system.

Key Takeaways

You're now able to successfully install an Ansible Control node, the "server" node that runs the automation, in all of the most used Linux and Enterprise Linux distributions, macOS, and Windows operating systems.

The newest Ansible package distribution policy (community vs. core) enables more flexible and space-efficient ways to deploy the Ansible platform and add only the relevant collections for your automation.

A lot of the most recent operating systems fully embrace this approach, and the list goes on and on.

In the following chapter, you are going to apply all the Ansible language code knowledge to automate the VMware infrastructure via code nutshells and commands snippets. By automating simple and complex tasks, you're going to save time and build an Infrastructure as Code (IaC) by applying DevOps methodologies.

## CHAPTER 3

Ansible for VMware

By now, you probably understand that Ansible is a phenomenal tool for automating system administrator tasks. In this chapter, the key focus is on the VMware infrastructure. I'm going to share with you some day-to-day use cases to save time and reduce errors. In the following pages, you're going to learn about the most important Ansible modules and plugins to automate your VMware infrastructure. There is code to specifically interact with VMware data centers, clusters, host systems, and virtual machines. By the end of this chapter, you are going to be able to automate mundane activities like spinning up a virtual machine or adding a second hard drive with a few lines of code.

Configuring Ansible for VMware

All Ansible resources to interact with the VMware infrastructure are packed inside the Ansible collection `community.vmware`. The resources are written in Python, as is Ansible, and require some Python dependency in order to work. The main dependency of the collection is `pyVmomi`, the Python SDK for the VMware vSphere API that allows you to connect and manage VMware ESX, ESXi, and the vCenter infrastructure. Each of the Ansible modules interacts with a specific element of the VMware infrastructure: data center, cluster, host system, and virtual machine. I'll show you step by step how to prepare your Ansible controller to interact with the VMware infrastructure. This initial configuration can be a roadblock for some VMware users to start using Ansible.

Please refer to the following sections to troubleshoot the most common Ansible for VMware errors and how to fix them:

- VMware failed to import `pyVmomi`

- VMware unknown error while connecting to vCenter or ESXi

- VMware certificate verification failed connecting to vCenter or ESXi

© Luca Berton 2023
L. Berton, *Ansible for VMware by Examples*, https://doi.org/10.1007/978-1-4842-8879-5_3

The Ansible vmware.vmware_rest Collection

The `vmware.vmware_rest` Ansible collection is an alternative to the `community.vmware` collection based upon the VMware vSphere REST API interface and does not rely on any third-party libraries such as `pyVmomi` and vSphere Automation SDK for Python. It does require the `aiohttp` Python library for Python 3.6 or greater.

The `vmware.vmware_rest` collection, at the moment of writing this book, is focused only on the life cycle of a VMware virtual machine and managing VMware vCenter server appliance (VCSA) automation resources.

The collection is supported by the Ansible VMware community and includes the VMware modules and plugins to help the management of the VMware infrastructure but at the moment offers limited automation options.

Read more about the `vmware.vmware_rest` collection in the website documentation .

This book covers the `community.vmware` collection that at the moment offers more automation resources.

The Ansible community.vmware Collection

- VMware vSphere 7.0, 6.0, 5.5, 5.1 and 5.0

The supported nodes include all the modern releases of VMware vSphere. The full list includes the latest releases of vSphere as well as 7.0, 6.0, 5.5, 5.1, and 5.0. The Ansible `community.vmware` VMware collection requires the Python `pyVmomi` library. `pyVmomi` is a software development kit (SDK) that interacts with the VMware vSphere API, enabling you to manage ESX, ESXi and the vCenter infrastructure in order to execute the Ansible automation.

- Python `pyVmomi` supports 2.7.x and 3.4+.

- Ansible collection `community.vmware`

The Ansible collection `community.vmware` contains modules and plugins packed with a lot of useful automation to perform any tasks and operations in your VMware infrastructure. Please consider taking a look at the official documentation because it's an evolving collection. Note that the `community.vmware` Ansible collection, as the name suggests, is provided by community support, so it's not directly maintained by the Ansible Engineer Team. The community-supported collection receives best-effort support from volunteer Ansible developers and creators. You can contribute as much as you like in the open source spirit.

Links

- Introduction to Ansible for VMware, https://docs.ansible.com/
  ansible/latest/scenario_guides/vmware_scenarios/vmware_
  intro.html

- community.vmware.vmware_guest_info, https://docs.ansible.
  com/ansible/latest/collections/community/vmware/vmware_
  guest_info_module.html

Code

Please allow me to guide you through the three main steps of automating your VMware infrastructure using Ansible. I'm going to share with you all the relevant resources to be successful on your Ansible journey from the beginning. Let's consider the use case of gathering information about a VMware virtual machine using the Ansible Playbook. Here's how to configure Ansible for VMware:

1. Install pyVmomi.

First, you need to install pyVmomi, the VMware vSphere API Python Bindings.

Don't panic! The first time you try to execute an Ansible Playbook on a system without the required pyVmomi Python library, you will receive a fatal error. This error may also indicate that Ansible is not able to locate the Python library in the current Python virtual environment or Ansible execution environment. Whenever the pyVmomi Python library is missing, the execution terminates with a **FAILED** status and you will see the following **fatal** error and description:

```
An exception occurred during task execution. To see the full traceback,
use -vvv. The error was: ModuleNotFoundError: No module named 'pyVim'
"Failed to import the required Python library (pyVmomi ) on demo.example.
com's Python /usr/libexec/platform-python. Please read module documentation
and install in the appropriate location. If the required library is
installed, but Ansible is using the wrong Python interpreter, please
consult the documentation on ansible_python_interpreter"
```

You can use PIP, the Python Package Manager, to install the required pyVmomi Python library. Please note that you may need to adjust the command based on the Python version running on your system. For example, `pip3` for Python 3, `pip3.9` for Python 3.9. Some distributions require installation of the `python3-pip` package. The following command installs the pyVmomi Python library system-wide using `root` privileges:

```
# pip install pyVmomi
```

Under the hood, PIP takes care of all the necessary Python dependencies: `requests`, `six`, `chardet`, `idna`, and `urllib3`.

After this command, you should have pyVmomi successfully installed on your system and you're ready to move to the following step.

2. Install the `community.vmware` collection.

Second, you need to install the Ansible `community.vmware` collection. The best Ansible way is via a `requirements.yml` file. You can also perform it manually using the `ansible-galaxy` command, but I prefer to automate as much as possible of my workflow. You can also insert this code in a script or Ansible Playbook. The Ansible `requirements.yml` file allows you to specify all the Ansible Collections or Ansible Roles that you want to install. In this use case, it's just simply a YAML document with the name of the `community.vmware` collection.

- requirements.yml

```
---
collections:
  - name: community.vmware
```

The execution is pretty smooth via the `ansible-galaxy` tool:

```
$ ansible-galaxy install -r requirements.yml
```

After this command, the `community.vmware` collection will be successfully installed in your system and you're ready to fully execute your Ansible code.

3. Ansible code, inventory, and Playbook

Once everything is done on the node, you can configure the Ansible inventory on the Ansible controller machine and run your first Ansible Playbook with the `vmware_guest_info` module to verify the successful configuration.

The Ansible inventory is super simple and is limited to localhost because the Ansible controller is going to connect to the VMware infrastructure via the VMware API.

- Inventory

localhost

The vm_info.yml Ansible Playbook simply gathers the VMware virtual machine details from the VMware infrastructure and prints them on screen. The variables used inside the Ansible Playbook are defined in the vars.yml file. It's a good test because you can connect to the VMware infrastructure, request some information with a parameter (the virtual machine name) to the VMware API, and return some information in a JSON format. You can process this information and execute more automation or simply print on screen like in this example.

- vm_info.yml

```
---
- name: info vm demo
  hosts: localhost

  gather_facts: false
  collections:
    - community.vmware
  pre_tasks:
    - include_vars: vars.yml
  tasks:
    - name: get VM info
      vmware_guest_info:
        hostname: "{{ vcenter_hostname }}"
        username: "{{ vcenter_username }}"
        password: "{{ vcenter_password }}"
        datacenter: "{{ vcenter_datacenter }}"
        validate_certs: "{{ vcenter_validate_certs }}"
        name: "{{ vm_name }}"
      register: detailed_vm_info
    - name: print VM info
      ansible.builtin.debug:
        var: detailed_vm_info
```

I prefer to store all the connection parameters in a separate `vars.yml` Ansible Playbook file that can be shared among different Ansible Playbook files. I strongly recommend you encrypt this document as an Ansible Vault because there is the username and password to connect to your VMware infrastructure.

- `vars.yml`

```
---
vcenter_hostname: "vmware.example.com"
vcenter_datacenter: "vmwaredatacenter"
vcenter_validate_certs: false
vcenter_username: "username@vsphere.local"
vcenter_password: "MySecretPassword123"
vm_name: "myvm"
```

These are simple variables used in the Ansible Playbook that you must customize to reflect the one actually used in your VMware infrastructure. The variable `vcenter_hostname` contains the hostname or IP address of your VMware ESXi or vCenter. The variable `vcenter_datacenter` contains the name of the data center, for example, `vmwaredatacenter`. The variable `vcenter_validate_certs` is a boolean that enables `true` or disables `false` for the SSL certificate validation. I disabled the SSL certificate validation in order to use a self-signed certificate in my infrastructure. I encourage you to use a valid SSL certificate or insert the local certification authority in the chain of trust of your system. The variable `vcenter_username` contains the username to connect to your VMware infrastructure. When it's a local username, you should append the suffix `@vsphere.local` or use an LDAP/ActiveDirectory credential. The variable `vcenter_password` contains the password used for the connection. Please be very careful about the case and special characters. You might need to escape some of them to use with Ansible. The variable `vm_name` contains the name of the virtual machine that you would like to get information about. In this example, it's `myvm`. Feel free to customize your code or use an extra variable in the command line.

When the previous steps are successful, the Ansible execution is super smooth and you will see onscreen all the details of your `myvm` VMware virtual machine.

The output includes

- Target host: `localhost`

- Command result: `ok=3`

- Return value: A long JSON output

The most important key is `instance` where you can read all the relevant information about the VMware virtual machine. Let me give you one example:

- Running server: "hw_esxi_host": "vmware.example.com"

- Running cluster: `"hw_cluster": "prod-cluster"

- Virtual machine name:"hw_name": "myvm"

- Motion id: "moid": "vm-17923"

- Instance UUID: "hw_product_uuid": "4225a846-b176-892d-0e27-10a4106269a0"

- Number of CPU processors: "hw_processor_count": 1

- Number of CPU cores: "hw_cores_per_socket": 1

- RAM resources: "hw_memtotal_mb": 1024

- Datastore name:

  ```
  "hw_datastores": [
      "Datastore-1"
  ],
  ```

- Datastore directory: "hw_folder": "/vmwaredatacenter/vm/myvm"

- Datastore files:

  ```
  "hw_files": [
      "[Datastore-1] myvm/myvm.vmx",
      "[Datastore-1] myvm/myvm.vmsd",
      "[Datastore-1] myvm/myvm.vmdk"
  ],
  ```

- Network interfaces and status:

  ```
  "hw_interfaces": [
      "eth0"
  ]
  "hw_eth0": { ... }
  ```

- Status of VMware Guest Tools: "guest_tools_status": guestToolsNotRunning"

Maybe this doesn't sound so exciting, but from now on you can execute any Ansible automation against your VMware infrastructure without any further interaction with VMware vSphere user interface or the complex VMware API. You're officially taking your first steps inside the Ansible for VMware infrastructure automation. I'm sure that you are already thinking about how you can automate the most boring task you're executing again and again, each day.

Configuring a Python Virtual Environment for Ansible VMware

Using a Python virtual environment is a convenient way to use the Ansible for VMware resources without interfering with your operating system. It's very useful when you want to use the latest releases not yet available as a package or a specific version of the resources. It's also a nice way to maintain the `community.vmware` Ansible collection and the related Python libraries' dependencies without interfering with your operating system. A Python virtual environment is a confined space created by Python where you can use a specific version of the Python libraries and resources. Configure your Python virtual environment for Ansible VMware `community.vmware` collection to use the latest releases of Python 3.8 with the latest `pyVmomi` and VMware vSphere Automation SDK for Python libraries. This initial configuration is sometimes a roadblock for some VMware users to start using Ansible.

Links

- Ansible collection community.vmware, `https://docs.ansible.com/ansible/latest/collections/community/vmware/index.html`

- Python pyVmomi, `https://github.com/vmware/pyvmomi`

- VMware vSphere Automation SDK for Python, `https://github.com/vmware/vsphere-automation-sdk-python`

Code

In order to successfully use the Ansible collection called `community.vmware` of modules and plugins to manage various operations related to virtual machines in the given ESXi or vCenter server, you can configure a Python virtual environment. These two are the main Python dependencies to handle in your Python virtual environment for Ansible VMware:

- pyVmomi: VMware vSphere API Python bindings

- vsphere-automation-sdk-python: VMware vSphere Automation SDK for Python

The Ansible For VMware resources are written on top of the pyVmomi Python SDK for the VMware vSphere API that allows users to manage ESX, ESXi, and the vCenter infrastructure. Another useful library is VMware vSphere Automation SDK for Python; it is used for additional features such as list tags in the Ansible dynamic inventory vmware_vm_inventory plugin. This example uses Python 3.8 so the pip3.8 tool adapts to your current configuration. Some Linux distributions require the installation of the python-pip or python3-pip package in order to provide the PIP tool. Please adjust python3.8 to python, python3, and python3.9 and pip3.8 to pip, pip3, and pip3.9 according to the running version in your system.

- configure-Python-venv.sh

```
$ python3.8 -m venv venv
$ source venv/bin/activate
(venv) $ pip3.8 install --upgrade pip setuptools
(venv) $ pip3.8 install --upgrade pyvmomi
(venv) $ pip3.8 install --upgrade vsphere-automation-sdk-python
```

The first command initializes a new Python virtual environment named venv using the Python module venv. You can customize the name as makes sense for you, but you should change it accordingly in the venv part of the activation script venv/bin/activate. You can leave the virtual environment at any time by typing the deactivate command. A prompt change with the Python virtual environment name (venv) between brackets is a common way to verify that you're actually operating inside the venv Python virtual environment. One good practice is to upgrade the PIP package manager to the latest available version and set up tools to easily manage the installation of packages and then proceed to install the Python resources. In this case, the pyVmomi and vsphere-automation-sdk-python Python libraries are installed.

If the installation of `vsphere-automation-sdk-python` library fails using the PIP package, you should rely on the GitHub archive. Substitute the last line with the following command:

```
(venv) $ pip3.8 install --upgrade git+https://github.com/vmware/vsphere-automation-sdk-python.git
```

The PIP package installer takes care of all the necessary Python dependencies:

- for pyVmomi: `six` and `requests`

- for vSphere-Automation-SDK-Python: `cffi`, `cryptography`, `lxml`, `nsx-policy-python-sdk`, `nsx-python-sdk`, `nsx-vmc-aws-integration-python-sdk`, `nsx-vmc-policy-python-sdk`, `pyOpenSSL`, `pycparser`, `vapi-client-bindings`, `vapi-common-client`, `vapi-runtime`, `vmc-client-bindings`, `vmc-draas-client-bindings`.

Once installed, you can produce a `requirements.txt` file, which is useful to share with other systems or recreate the Python virtual environment using the command

```
(venv) [devops@demo ~]$ pip3.8 freeze > requirements.txt
```

This is an example `requirements.txt` file for my Python virtual environment Ansible For VMware:

- requirements.txt

  ```
  certifi==2022.6.15
  cffi==1.15.1
  charset-normalizer==2.1.1
  cryptography==37.0.4
  idna==3.3
  lxml==4.9.1
  nsx-policy-python-sdk @ file://localhost//tmp/pip-req-
  build-lvOgh9o2/lib/nsx-policy-python-sdk/nsx_policy_python_
  sdk-4.0.0.0.0-py2.py3-none-any.whl
  nsx-python-sdk @ file://localhost//tmp/pip-req-build-lvOgh9o2/lib/
  nsx-python-sdk/nsx_python_sdk-4.0.0.0.0-py2.py3-none-any.whl
  ```

```
nsx-vmc-aws-integration-python-sdk @ file://localhost//tmp/pip-
req-build-lv0gh902/lib/nsx-vmc-aws-integration-python-sdk/nsx_vmc_
aws_integration_python_sdk-4.0.0.0.0-py2.py3-none-any.whl
nsx-vmc-policy-python-sdk @ file://localhost//tmp/pip-req-build-
lv0gh902/lib/nsx-vmc-policy-python-sdk/nsx_vmc_policy_python_
sdk-4.0.0.0.0-py2.py3-none-any.whl
pycparser==2.21
pyOpenSSL==22.0.0
pyvmomi==7.0.3
requests==2.28.1
six==1.16.0
urllib3==1.26.12
vapi-client-bindings @ file://localhost//tmp/pip-req-build-
lv0gh902/lib/vapi-client-bindings/vapi_client_bindings-3.9.0-py2.
py3-none-any.whl
vapi-common-client @ file://localhost//tmp/pip-req-build-lv0gh902/
lib/vapi-common-client/vapi_common_client-2.34.0-py2.py3-
none-any.whl
vapi-runtime @ file://localhost//tmp/pip-req-build-lv0gh902/lib/
vapi-runtime/vapi_runtime-2.34.0-py2.py3-none-any.whl
vmc-client-bindings @ file://localhost//tmp/pip-req-build-
lv0gh902/lib/vmc-client-bindings/vmc_client_bindings-1.60.0-py2.
py3-none-any.whl
vmc-draas-client-bindings @ file://localhost//tmp/pip-req-
build-lv0gh902/lib/vmc-draas-client-bindings/vmc_draas_client_
bindings-1.19.0-py2.py3-none-any.whl
vSphere-Automation-SDK==1.78.0
```

Ansible Troubleshooting: VMware Failed to Import pyVmomi

You may obtain the Failed to import the required Python library (pyVmomi)
fatal error when you try to execute your Ansible Playbook code. This error is incredibly
common. This fatal error message happens when the Ansible control node is not able
to execute your Ansible Playbook code. This fatal error message happens when you

try to execute some code against your VMware infrastructure without the necessary Python SDK for the VMware vSphere API. The `community.vmware` Ansible collection requires the **pyVmomi** Python SDK library to be installed on the Ansible controller in order to execute the code. The root cause may be related to Ansible not being able to locate the correct path for the Python library or the missing library at all. The library can be installed system-wide, per user, in a Python virtual environment, or in an Ansible execution environment. You should use PIP to take care of the installation and maintain the pyVmomi Python library in your system. These circumstances are usually related to the configuration of your Ansible controller node and usually are not related to an Ansible Playbook.

Code

Let me show you how to reproduce, troubleshoot, and fix the Ansible fatal error `ModuleNotFoundError: No module named 'pyVim'"`.

In this example, execute the code in an Ansible controller without the pyVmomi Python SDK library installed. I'll demonstrate this behavior using the vm_info.yml Ansible Playbook that gathers the myvm VMware virtual machine details from the VMware infrastructure and prints them on screen. The first execution leads to an (expected) failure because the pyVmomi Python SDK library is missing. Then you can install the necessary Python dependency using the PIP tool. The second execution of the same code returns a successful execution.

- vm_info.yml

```
---

- name: info vm demo
  hosts: localhost

  gather_facts: false
  collections:
    - community.vmware
  pre_tasks:
    - include_vars: vars.yml
  tasks:
    - name: get VM info
```

```
        vmware_guest_info:
          hostname: "{{ vcenter_hostname }}"
          username: "{{ vcenter_username }}"
          password: "{{ vcenter_password }}"
          datacenter: "{{ vcenter_datacenter }}"
          validate_certs: "{{ vcenter_validate_certs }}"
          name: "{{ vm_name }}"
        register: detailed_vm_info

    - name: print VM info
      ansible.builtin.debug:
        var: detailed_vm_info
```

The Ansible inventory is only the `localhost` because you're executing the Ansible automation on the Ansible controller.

- Inventory

```
localhost
```

The `vars.yml` file stores all the VMware infrastructure connection parameters that may be shared among different Ansible Playbook files.

- vars.yml

```
---
vcenter_hostname: "vm-ware.example.com"
vcenter_datacenter: "vmwaredatacenter"
vcenter_validate_certs: false
vcenter_username: "username@vsphere.local"
vcenter_password: "MySecretPassword123"
vm_name: "myvm"
```

In an unsuccessful execution, the output is

- Target host: `localhost`

- Command result: `failed=1`

- Return value:

```
fatal: [localhost]: FAILED! => {"ansible_facts": {"discovered_
interpreter_python": "/usr/libexec/platform-python"}, "changed":
false, "msg": "Failed to import the required Python library
(pyVmomi ) on demo.example.com's Python /usr/libexec/platform-
python. Please read module documentation and install in the
appropriate location. If the required library is installed, but
Ansible is using the wrong Python interpreter, please consult the
documentation on ansible_python_interpreter"}
```

The fatal error message gives you the full path of the system-wise running Python interpreter (/usr/libexec/platform-python specifically). So, you need to perform the installation of pyVmomi in the currently running user or system wide. The fix requires you to install the missing pyVmomi Python library in the right place in your system.

Sometimes the root cause of the failure is the permission bits for newly created files. Some high-security systems have strict non-standard settings via a global /etc/profile file or .bashrc inside the user's home directory.

The standard POSIX utility umask allows you to set the octal value to set the permission for new files.

The Ansible Engineer Team highly recommends that you run umask 0022 before installing any packages to the virtual environment.

The default umask 0022 result into a newly created directory called permissions is 755 and file permissions is 644.

The two options to install the pyVmomi Python library are

- Install pyVmomi system wide.

  `# pip install pyVmomi`

- Install pyVmomi for a user.

  `$ pip install --user pyVmomi`

Please adjust the pip tool according to the version installed on your systems, such as pip3 for Python3 and pip3.9 for Python3.9. Some distributions require the installation of the python3-pip package. PIP takes care of downloading, installing, and verifying all the necessary dependencies: requests, six, chardet, idna, and urllib3.

Once the `pyVmomi` Python SDK library is installed in the system, the Ansible Playbook execution is successful with the following output:

- Target host: `localhost`

- Command result: `ok=3`

- Return value: A long JSON output of the `myvm` virtual machine

Please refer to "Configuring Ansible For VMware" for more details about the JSON output of the `vm_info.yml` Ansible Playbook.

Ansible Troubleshooting: VMware Unknown Error While Connecting to vCenter or ESXi

You may obtain the `Unknown error while connecting to vCenter or ESXi` fatal error when you try to connect to your VMware infrastructure. This error is extremely common. The full message of the Ansible fatal error is `Unknown error while connecting to vCenter or ESXi API, [Errno -2] Name or service not known`. This fatal error message happens when the Ansible controller is not able to connect to your VMware infrastructure. The root cause might be a misspelled hostname in your Ansible Playbook, a connection problem, or eventually a secure VPN connection that is not enabled to reach the VMware vCenter/ESXi host or a configuration on the firewall on the target host. To summarize, it might be a code or network root cause. This is a typical roadblock that sometimes stops you from successfully running your Ansible For VMware Playbook code.

Code

Let me show you how to reproduce, troubleshoot, and fix the Ansible error `Unknown error while connecting to vCenter or ESXi API [Errno -2] Name or service not known`.

In this example, I'll introduce a very simple and common typo error in the hostname: `vm-ware.example.com` instead of the correct `vmware.example.com` of the VMware infrastructure. I always suggest using your browser to try to access the URL as a first test. You can easily test this host by copying and pasting the address and trying to reach the VMware vSphere web interface. If your browser returns a "host unavailable" message, it becomes clear that the hostname was misspelled. The issue may be more complex depending on your network topology and may require analyzing the network traffic between the Ansible controller and the target machine. Please verify the firewall, VPN, and other rules as well. Let me share with you the example with a misspelled hostname, `vm-ware.example.com` instead of the correct `vmware.example.com` of the VMware infrastructure, just a simple human typo mistake.

The `vm_info.yml` Ansible Playbook simply gathers the VMware virtual machine details from the VMware infrastructure and prints them on screen. The variables used inside the Ansible Playbook are defined in the `vars.yml` file.

- `vm_info.yml`

```
---
- name: info vm demo
  hosts: localhost

  gather_facts: false
  collections:
    - community.vmware
  pre_tasks:
    - include_vars: vars.yml
  tasks:
    - name: get VM info
      vmware_guest_info:
        hostname: "{{ vcenter_hostname }}"
        username: "{{ vcenter_username }}"
        password: "{{ vcenter_password }}"
        datacenter: "{{ vcenter_datacenter }}"
        validate_certs: "{{ vcenter_validate_certs }}"
        name: "{{ vm_name }}"
      register: detailed_vm_info

    - name: print VM info
      ansible.builtin.debug:
        var: detailed_vm_info
```

The Ansible inventory is only the `localhost` because you're executing the Ansible automation on the Ansible controller.

- Inventory

  `localhost`

The `vars.yml` file stores all the VMware infrastructure connection parameters that may be shared among different Ansible Playbook files.

- `vars.yml`

  ```
  ---
  vcenter_hostname: "vm-ware.example.com"
  vcenter_datacenter: "vmwaredatacenter"
  vcenter_validate_certs: false
  vcenter_username: "username@vsphere.local"
  vcenter_password: "MySecretPassword123"
  vm_name: "myvm"
  ```

In an unsuccessful execution, the output is

- Target host: `localhost`

- Command result: `failed=1`

- Return value:

  ```
  fatal: [localhost]: FAILED! => {"changed": false, "msg":
  "Unknown error while connecting to vCenter or ESXi API
  at vm-ware.example.com:443 : [Errno -2] Name or service
  not known"}
  ```

The fatal error message gives you the full hostname and port `vm-ware.example. com:443` user by Ansible. Just copy and paste the `vm-ware.example.com` hostname and port HTTPS (443) to spot the misspelling human error.

The fix is very easy and requires you to only modify the `vcenter_hostname` variable in the `vars.yml` file with the right hostname.

- `vars.yml`

  ```
  vcenter_hostname: "vmware.example.com"
  ```

Using the right hostname in the vcenter_hostname variable, the execution is successful with the following output:

- Target host: localhost

- Command result: ok=3

- Return value: A long JSON output of the myvm virtual machine

Please refer to "Configuring Ansible For VMware" for more details about the JSON output of the vm_info.yml Ansible Playbook.

Ansible Troubleshooting: VMware Certificate Verification Failed Connecting to vCenter or ESXi

You may obtain the Unable to connect to vCenter or ESXi API [SSL: CERTIFICATE_VERIFY_FAILED] certificate verify failed (_ssl.c:897) fatal error when you try to connect to your VMware infrastructure. This is a common error. The full message of the Ansible fatal error is Unable to connect to vCenter or ESXi API at vmware.example.com on TCP/443: [SSL: CERTIFICATE_VERIFY_FAILED] certificate verify failed (_ssl.c:897). The root cause is related to the SSL certificate validation necessary for encrypting the information shared via HTTPS connections to the VMware vSphere API. It might be an invalid SSL certificate, an invalid hostname, an inability to validate the chain of trust, or a self-signed SSL certificate. Ansible modules have the validate_certs boolean parameter to enable and disable the SSL certificate validation process. The most common scenario is to skip the validation of self-signed certificates, which ends with a fatal error regarding the certificate SSL validation. The easy fix is to disable the SSL certificate validation process in the Ansible Playbook or add the certificate chain of trust/certificate authority in the Ansible controlled system.

Code

Suppose your VMware infrastructure uses a self-signed certificate such as the one that came out of the box with the VMware. Let me show you what happens if you don't specify the validate_certs parameter for the Ansible module. The validate_certs boolean parameter defaults to true so Ansible will perform the certificate SSL validation.

Let me demonstrate this behavior using the `vm_info.yml` Ansible Playbook that gathers the `myvm` VMware virtual machine details from the VMware infrastructure and prints them on screen. The first execution leads to an (expected) failure because the `validate_certs` boolean parameter is missing, so it defaults to `true`. Then you correct the Ansible Playbook to include the `validate_certs` boolean parameter with the `false` value to disable the certificate SSL validation. The second execution of the code returns a successful execution.

Error Code

- `vm_info_error.yml`

```
---

- name: info vm demo
  hosts: localhost

  gather_facts: false
  collections:
    - community.vmware
  pre_tasks:
    - include_vars: vars.yml
  tasks:
    - name: get VM info
      vmware_guest_info:
        hostname: "{{ vcenter_hostname }}"
        username: "{{ vcenter_username }}"
        password: "{{ vcenter_password }}"
        datacenter: "{{ vcenter_datacenter }}"
        name: "{{ vm_name }}"
      register: detailed_vm_info
    - name: print VM info
      ansible.builtin.debug:
        var: detailed_vm_info
```

The vars.yml file stores all the VMware infrastructure connection parameters that may be shared among different Ansible Playbook files.

- vars.yml

```
---
vcenter_hostname: "vmware.example.com"
vcenter_datacenter: "vmwaredatacenter"
vcenter_username: "username@vsphere.local"
vcenter_password: "MySecretPassword123"
vm_name: "myvm"
```

The Ansible inventory is only the localhost because you're executing the Ansible automation on the Ansible controller.

- Inventory

  localhost

In an unsuccessful execution, the output is

- Target host: localhost

- Command result: failed=1

- Return value:

```
TASK [get VM info]
fatal: [localhost]: FAILED! => {"changed": false, "msg":
"Unable to connect to vCenter or ESXi API at vmware.
example.com on TCP/443: [SSL: CERTIFICATE_VERIFY_FAILED]
certificate verify failed (_ssl.c:897)"}
```

Fixed Code

It's possible to avoid SSL certificate validation by setting the parameter validate_certs. For a self-signed certificate, you need to disable the SSL certificate validation. However, I strongly recommend creating a custom chain of trust or using a valid SSL certificate. The only change is the addition of the validate_certs parameter to the vmware_guest_info Ansible module using a vcenter_validate_certs variable defined in the vars.yml file.

- vm_info_fix.yml

```yaml
---
- name: info vm demo
  hosts: localhost

  gather_facts: false
  collections:
    - community.vmware
  pre_tasks:
    - include_vars: vars.yml
  tasks:
    - name: get VM info
      vmware_guest_info:
        hostname: "{{ vcenter_hostname }}"
        username: "{{ vcenter_username }}"
        password: "{{ vcenter_password }}"
        datacenter: "{{ vcenter_datacenter }}"
        validate_certs: "{{ vcenter_validate_certs }}"
        name: "{{ vm_name }}"
      register: detailed_vm_info
    - name: print VM info
      ansible.builtin.debug:
        var: detailed_vm_info
```

The new vars.yml also includes the vcenter_validate_certs variable set to false to disable the SSL certificate validation process.

- vars.yml

```yaml
---
vcenter_hostname: "vmware.example.com"
vcenter_datacenter: "vmwaredatacenter"
vcenter_username: "username@vsphere.local"
vcenter_password: "MySecretPassword123"
vcenter_validate_certs: false
vm_name: "myvm"
```

Once the `validate_certs` is set to false, the Ansible Playbook execution is successful with the following output:

- Target host: `localhost`

- Command result: `ok=3`

- Return value: A long JSON output of the `myvm` virtual machine

Please refer to "Configuring Ansible For VMware" for more details about the JSON output of the `vm_info.yml` Ansible Playbook.

Creating a VMware Virtual Machine

You can automate the creation of a VMware virtual machine guest using an Ansible Playbook and the `vmware_guest` module. The creation of a VMware virtual machine is one of the most mundane activities for a system administrator. It's also one of the most error-prone, because traditionally it requires some human interaction in the VMware vSphere user interface. The traditional way of creating a virtual machine requires filling out some forms in the vSphere client or web user interface. These forms may sound complex for early adopters because they are designed for a lot of use cases so they have plenty of options inside. For example, let's create a Linux virtual machine running a 64-bit operating system with the following assigned resources: 1 CPU, 1GB RAM, and 10GB of thin-provisioned storage (see Figure 3-1).

Ansible vmware_guest Module

- `community.vmware.vmware_guest`

The Ansible module `vmware_guest` is used to interact with your VMware infrastructure and create or manage VMware virtual machines. The full name is `community.vmware.vmware_guest`, which means that it is part of the collection of modules that interact with VMware and is community supported. The module `vmware_guest` has a very long list of parameters to customize all your needs to create a VMware vSphere virtual machine. The resource allocation list is especially extended to cover the more possible use cases. I suggest you begin with a minimum solution and then improve it little by little until you reach your expected outcome. It may be difficult to troubleshoot several lines of code and options at a time. Please refer to the manual for the full list.

Links

- community.vmware.vmware_guest, https://docs.ansible.com/
  ansible/latest/collections/community/vmware/vmware_guest_
  module.html

Code

Here's the code to create a virtual machine named myvm with the following resources (see Figure 3-1):

- 1 CPU

- 1GB of RAM

- 10GB of thin-provisioned storage in the datastore named Datastore-1
  network card named VM Network of type vmxnet3

- create_vm.yml

```
---
- name: create vm demo
  hosts: localhost

  gather_facts: false
  collections:
    - community.vmware
  pre_tasks:
    - include_vars: vars.yml
  tasks:
    - name: create VM folder
      vcenter_folder:
        hostname: "{{ vcenter_hostname }}"
        username: "{{ vcenter_username }}"
        password: "{{ vcenter_password }}"
        validate_certs: "{{ vcenter_validate_certs }}"
        datacenter_name: "{{ vcenter_datacenter }}"
        folder_name: "{{ vcenter_destination_folder }}"
        folder_type: vm
        state: present
```

```
- name: create VM
  vmware_guest:
    hostname: "{{ vcenter_hostname }}"
    username: "{{ vcenter_username }}"
    password: "{{ vcenter_password }}"
    validate_certs: "{{ vcenter_validate_certs }}"
    datacenter: "{{ vcenter_datacenter }}"
    name: "{{ vm_name }}"
    folder: "{{ vcenter_destination_folder }}"
    state: "{{ vm_state }}"
    guest_id: "{{ vm_guestid }}"
    cluster: "{{ vcenter_cluster }}"
    disk:
      - size_gb: "{{ vm_disk_gb }}"
        type: "{{ vm_disk_type }}"
        datastore: "{{ vm_disk_datastore }}"
    hardware:
      memory_mb: "{{ vm_hw_ram_mb }}"
      num_cpus: "{{ vm_hw_cpu_n }}"
      scsi: "{{ vm_hw_scsi }}"
    networks:
      - name: "{{ vm_net_name }}"
        device_name: "{{ vm_net_type }}"
```

The vars.yml file stores all the VMware infrastructure connection parameters that may be shared among different Ansible Playbook files.

- vars.yml

```
---
vcenter_hostname: "vmware.example.com"
vcenter_datacenter: "vmwaredatacenter"
vcenter_validate_certs: false
vcenter_username: "username@vsphere.local"
vcenter_password: "MySecretPassword123"
vcenter_cluster: "Development"
```

```
vm_name: "myvm"
vm_guestid: "centos64Guest"
vm_disk_gb: 10
vm_disk_type: "thin"
vm_disk_datastore: "Datastore-1"
vm_hw_ram_mb: 1024
vm_hw_cpu_n: 1
vm_hw_scsi: "paravirtual"
vm_net_name: "VM Network"
vm_net_type: "vmxnet3"
vcenter_destination_folder: "myvm"
vm_state: "poweroff"
```

The Ansible inventory is only the localhost because you're executing the Ansible automation on the Ansible controller.

- Inventory

localhost

A successful execution output includes

- Target host: localhost

- Command result: ok=3

- Return value:

```
TASK [create VM folder]
changed: [localhost]
TASK [create VM]
changed: [localhost]
```

If the virtual machine is already present, the module return an "ok" status (the vmware_guest module is idempotent):

- Target host: localhost

- Command result: ok=3

- Return value:

```
TASK [create VM folder]
ok: [localhost]
TASK [create VM]
ok: [localhost]
```

After the execution of the code, you expect the following result in your VMware vSphere client user interface. See Figure 3-1.

Figure 3-1. *VMware virtual machine created with Ansible*

Deploying a VMware Virtual Machine from a Template

You can automate the deployment of a VMware virtual machine template using an Ansible Playbook and the `vmware_guest` module. A VMware virtual machine template is a previously created image that you can use as a master image to create more virtual machines in your VMware infrastructure. The template images simplify the provisioning process of guest virtual machines by using a previously prepared master image with the installed base operating system and the most used enterprise software. It's useful for the Microsoft Windows operating system because VMware takes care of the activation and serial number key under the hood. The deploying of a virtual machine from a template is one of the most repetitive activities for any person managing the VMware infrastructure. There is usually a copy from the template phase and a customization phase with some parameter specifications for customizing the guest operating system. This task usually requires some human interaction to complete some forms in the vSphere client or web user interface. This operation is sometimes error prone because it is human dependent.

Ansible Module vmware_guest

- `community.vmware.vmware_guest`

The Ansible module `vmware_guest` is used to interact with your VMware infrastructure and create or manage VMware virtual machines. The full name is `community.vmware.vmware_guest`, which means that it is part of the collection of modules that interact with VMware and is community supported. The module `vmware_guest` has a very long list of parameters to customize all your needs to create a VMware vSphere virtual machine. Please refer to the manual for the full list.

Links

- `community.vmware.vmware_guest`, `https://docs.ansible.com/ansible/latest/collections/community/vmware/vmware_guest_module.html`

Code

I'm going to show you how to deploy a virtual machine named `myvm` from a template `mytemplate` without any customization (see Figure 3-2). The Ansible Playbook includes the file `vars.yml` for some common variables for the VMware infrastructure and has two tasks for creating a virtual machine folder in the datastore and one for deploying the virtual machine from the template.

- `vm_deploy_template.yml`

```
---
- name: deploy vm from template demo
  hosts: localhost

  gather_facts: false
  collections:
    - community.vmware
  pre_tasks:
    - include_vars: vars.yml
  tasks:
    - name: create VM folder
      vcenter_folder:
```

```
          hostname: "{{ vcenter_hostname }}"
          username: "{{ vcenter_username }}"
          password: "{{ vcenter_password }}"
          validate_certs: "{{ vcenter_validate_certs }}"
          datacenter_name: "{{ vcenter_datacenter }}"
          folder_name: "{{ vcenter_destination_folder }}"
          folder_type: vm
          state: present
    - name: deploy VM from template
      vmware_guest:
          hostname: "{{ vcenter_hostname }}"
          username: "{{ vcenter_username }}"
          password: "{{ vcenter_password }}"
          validate_certs: "{{ vcenter_validate_certs }}"
          datacenter: "{{ vcenter_datacenter }}"
          cluster: "{{ vcenter_cluster }}"
          name: "{{ vm_name }}"
          folder: "{{ vcenter_destination_folder }}"
          template: "{{ vm_template }}"
```

The vars.yml file stores all the VMware infrastructure connection parameters that may be shared among different Ansible Playbook files.

- vars.yml

```
---
vcenter_hostname: "vmware.example.com"
vcenter_datacenter: "vmwaredatacenter"
vcenter_validate_certs: false
vcenter_username: "username@vsphere.local"
vcenter_password: "MySecretPassword123"
vcenter_cluster: "Development"
vm_name: "myvm"
vcenter_destination_folder: "myvm"
vm_state: "poweroff"
vm_template: "mytemplate"
```

The Ansible inventory is only the `localhost` because you're executing the Ansible automation on the Ansible controller.

- Inventory

  `localhost`

A successful execution output includes

- Target host: `localhost`

- Command result: `ok=3`

- Return value:

```
TASK [create VM folder]
changed: [localhost]
TASK [deploy VM from template]
changed: [localhost]
```

After the execution of the code, you expect the following result in your VMware vSphere client user interface. See Figure 3-2.

Figure 3-2. *Deploying a VMware virtual machine from a template with Ansible*

Starting a VMware Virtual Machine

You can automate the startup of a VMware virtual machine guest using an Ansible Playbook and the `vmware_guest_powerstate` module. Some organizations turn off virtual machines to manage off-peak and on-peak moments, for backup purposes, overnight maintenance, or for environmental reasons. Whatever your why, Ansible can automate the virtual machine lifecycle with few lines of code. The management of the power state transition of a VMware virtual machine is one of the most mundane activities for a VMware infrastructure administrator. The traditional way of manually changing the power state of a virtual machine requires you to access the vSphere client or web user interface. This procedure might be error-prone if you turn on or off the wrong virtual machine. For example, let's automate the transition from Powered Off to Powered On of the virtual machine guest `myvm` using an Ansible Playbook and the `vmware_guest_powerstate` module (see Figure 3-3 for before the execution and Figure 3-4 for after the execution).

Ansible Module vmware_guest_powerstate

- `community.vmware.vmware_guest_powerstate`

You can manage the power state of any virtual machine in your VMware infrastructure using the Ansible module `vmware_guest_powerstate`. The full name of the `vmware_guest_powerstate` module is `community.vmware.vmware_guest_powerstate`, which means that it is part of the collection of modules that interact with VMware and is community supported. It manages the power states of virtual machines in vCenter.

Parameters

- hostname *string*/port *integer*/username *string*/password *string*/datacenter *string*/validate_certs *boolean*: Connection details

- state *string*: present/powered-off/powered-on/reboot-guest/restarted/shutdown-guest/suspended

- force *boolean*: No/yes

- answer *string*: A list of questions to answer, should one or more arise while waiting for the task to be complete

The following parameters are useful in order to start a VMware vSphere virtual machine using the module vmware_guest_powerstate. First, you need to establish the connection with VMware vSphere or VMware vCenter using a plethora of self-explanatory parameters: hostname, port, username, password, datacenter, and validate_certs. Once the connection is successfully established, you can specify the desired power state, in this case, powered-on. You can also force the power state change using the force parameter (default: disabled). You can also specify the reply to some answer that can arise while waiting for the task to complete. Some common uses are to allow a CD-ROM to be changed even if locked or to answer the question as to whether a VM was copied or moved.

Links

- community.vmware.vmware_guest_powerstate, https://docs. ansible.com/ansible/latest/collections/community/vmware/ vmware_guest_powerstate_module.html

Code

I'm going to show you how to start the virtual machine named myvm from the power state Powered Off to the power state Powered On using an Ansible Playbook. The Ansible Playbook includes the file vars.yml for some common variables for the VMware infrastructure and has one task for powering one of the virtual machine with the specified name myvm. Under the hood, Ansible interacts with the VMware API via Python libraries to execute the operation and verify the successful startup of the virtual machine.

- vm_start.yml

```
---
- name: start vm demo
  hosts: localhost

  gather_facts: false
  collections:
    - community.vmware
  pre_tasks:
    - include_vars: vars.yml
```

```
      tasks:
      - name: power on VM
          vmware_guest_powerstate:
            hostname: "{{ vcenter_hostname }}"
            username: "{{ vcenter_username }}"
            password: "{{ vcenter_password }}"
            name: "{{ vm_name }}"
            validate_certs: "{{ vcenter_validate_certs }}"
            state: powered-on
```

The vars.yml file stores all the VMware infrastructure connection parameters that may be shared among different Ansible Playbook files.

- vars.yml

```
---
vcenter_hostname: "vmware.example.com"
vcenter_datacenter: "vmwaredatacenter"
vcenter_validate_certs: false
vcenter_username: "username@vsphere.local"
vcenter_password: "MySecretPassword123"
vm_name: "myvm"
```

The Ansible inventory is only the localhost because you're executing the Ansible automation on the Ansible controller.

- Inventory

  localhost

A successful execution output includes

- Target host: localhost

- Command result: ok=2 changed=1

- Return value:

  ```
  TASK [power on VM]
  changed: [localhost]
  ```

If the virtual machine guest is already in the powered-on status, the execution output includes

- Target host: `localhost`

- Command result: `ok=2`

- Return value:

  ```
  TASK [power on VM]
  ok: [localhost]
  ```

You can see the result of the startup of the VMware virtual machine in the VMware vSphere Web User interface. See Figures 3-3 and 3-4.

Figure 3-3. *Before starting a VMware virtual machine*

Figure 3-4. *After starting a VMware virtual machine*

Stopping a VMware Virtual Machine

You can automate the shutdown of a VMware virtual machine guest by using an Ansible Playbook and the `vmware_guest_powerstate` module. If your enterprise is used to turning off some virtual machines off-peak for backup purposes, overnight maintenance, or environmental reasons, you can benefit from the Ansible automation platform. You can easily automate the virtual machine lifecycle with a few lines of code, one of the boring activities for a VMware infrastructure administrator. You're probably familiar with the manual way: the one that requires to access the vSphere client or web user interface in order to turn off a virtual machine. Please note that you should be very careful to turn off the right virtual machine. Moreover, virtual machines sometimes need to be forced to shut down when the operating system doesn't support ACPI, there is a problem with the guest operating system, or simply if doesn't work on the first try. Let's automate the graceful guest shutdown and forceful power off to change the power state from Powered On to Powered Off of the virtual machine guest myvm using an Ansible Playbook and the `vmware_guest_powerstate` module (see Figure 3-5 for before the execution and Figure 3-6 for after the execution).

Ansible Module vmware_guest_powerstate

- `community.vmware.vmware_guest_powerstate`

You can manage the power state of any virtual machine in your VMware infrastructure using the Ansible module `vmware_guest_powerstate`. The full name of the `vmware_guest_powerstate` module is `community.vmware.vmware_guest_powerstate`, which means that it is part of the collection of modules that interact with VMware and is community supported. It manages the power states of virtual machines in vCenter.

Parameters

- hostname *string*/port *integer*/username *string*/password *string*/ datacenter *string*/validate_certs *boolean*: Connection details

- state *string* - present/powered-off/powered-on/reboot-guest/ restarted/shutdown-guest/suspended

- force *boolean*: No/yes

- answer *string*: A list of questions to answer, should one or more arise while waiting for the task to be complete

The following parameters are useful in order to start a VMware vSphere virtual machine using the module `vmware_guest_powerstate`. First, you need to establish a connection with VMware vSphere or VMware vCenter using a plethora of self-explanatory parameters: `hostname`, `port`, `username`, `password`, `datacenter`, and `validate_certs`. Once the connection is successfully established, you can specify the desired power state, in this case, `shutdown-guest` to gracefully ask the guest operating system to shut down or `powered-off` to turn off the virtual machine guest. You can also force the power state to change using the `force` parameter (default: disabled).

Links

- community.vmware.vmware_guest_powerstate, `https://docs.ansible.com/ansible/latest/collections/community/vmware/vmware_guest_powerstate_module.html`

Code

Here's how to get the virtual machine named `myvm` from the power state Powered On to the power state Powered Off using an Ansible Playbook (see Figure 3-5 for before the execution and Figure 3-6 for after the execution). Let's first try the `shutdown-guest` operation to gracefully ask the guest operating system to shut down and then `powered-off` to forcefully turn off the virtual machine guest. The Ansible Playbook includes the file `vars.yml` for some common variables for the VMware infrastructure and has one task for powering one of the virtual machine with the specified name `myvm`. Under the hood, Ansible interacts with the VMware API via Python libraries to execute the operation and verify the successful startup of the virtual machine. A timeout of 120 seconds (2 minutes) is set for the guest shutdown task; the default of the `vmware_guest_powerstate` module returns immediately (value 0) after sending the shutdown signal.

- vm_stop.yml

```
---

- name: stop vm demo
  hosts: localhost

  gather_facts: false
  collections:
    - community.vmware
```

```
    pre_tasks:
      - include_vars: vars.yml
    tasks:
      - name: guest shutdown
        vmware_guest_powerstate:
          hostname: "{{ vcenter_hostname }}"
          username: "{{ vcenter_username }}"
          password: "{{ vcenter_password }}"
          validate_certs: "{{ vcenter_validate_certs }}"
          name: "{{ vm_name }}"
          state: shutdown-guest
          state_change_timeout: 120
        register: shutdown
        ignore_errors: true

      - name: poweroff
        vmware_guest_powerstate:
          hostname: "{{ vcenter_hostname }}"
          username: "{{ vcenter_username }}"
          password: "{{ vcenter_password }}"
          validate_certs: "{{ vcenter_validate_certs }}"
          name: "{{ vm_name }}"
          state: powered-off
        when: shutdown.failed
```

The vars.yml file stores all the VMware infrastructure connection parameters that may be shared among different Ansible Playbook files.

- vars.yml

```
---
vcenter_hostname: "vmware.example.com"
vcenter_datacenter: "vmwaredatacenter"
vcenter_validate_certs: false
vcenter_username: "username@vsphere.local"
vcenter_password: "MySecretPassword123"
vm_name: "myvm"
```

The Ansible inventory is only the `localhost` because you're executing the Ansible automation on the Ansible controller.

- Inventory

  `localhost`

Three possible scenarios for the virtual machine shutdown might happen: a gentle guest shutdown, a power off, or an already powered-off status.

Successful execution of the guest shutdown output produces

- Target host: `localhost`

- Command result: `ok=2 changed=1`

- Return value:

  ```
  TASK [guest shutdown]
  changed: [localhost]
  ```

If the guest shutdown operation is unsuccessful any reason, the execution moves to the power-off operation, which produces

- Target host: `localhost`

- Command result: `ok=3 changed=1`

- Return value:

  ```
  TASK [guest shutdown]
  fatal: [localhost]: FAILED! => {"msg": "VMware tools should be
  installed for guest shutdown/reboot"}
  ...ignoring
  TASK [poweroff]
  changed: [localhost]
  ```

If the guest is already in the power-off state, the shutdown operation returns the following:

- Target host: `localhost`

- Command result: `ok=3`

- Return value:

```
TASK [guest shutdown]
fatal: [localhost]: FAILED! => {"msg": "Virtual machine
myvm must be in poweredon state for guest shutdown/
reboot"}
...ignoring
TASK [poweroff]
ok: [localhost]
```

You can see the result of the shutdown of the VMware virtual machine in the VMware vSphere web user interface in Figures 3-5 and 3-6.

Figure 3-5. *Before stopping a VMware virtual machine*

Figure 3-6. *After stopping a VMware virtual machine*

Taking a VMware Virtual Machine Snapshot

You can automate the process of taking snapshots of a VMware virtual machine by using an Ansible Playbook and the `vmware_guest_snapshot` module. VMware virtual machine snapshots are a convenient way of storing a particular state of a virtual machine in time. Virtualization enables you to take snapshots also at runtime. Some enterprise backup solutions such as Veeam Backup and Replication rely on the VMware snapshot feature. The traditional way of manually taking a snapshot of a virtual machine requires access the vSphere client or web user interface. It requires several interactions with the user interface in order to execute one VMware snapshot. From the Ansible point of view, the `vmware_guest_snapshot` module identifies the virtual machine by the name `myvm` in this example, and you can also define the desired snapshot name, for example, Ansible Managed Snapshot, for an easier way to find it. When snapshots starts to pile up, you will definitely love the name and description feature! If you prefer a date and time notation, use the `ansible_date_time` Ansible fact variable. In particular, for the ISO 8601 notation, the global standard for date and time, the notation just specifies `ansible_date_time.iso8601` in your Ansible Playbook and obtains a value like 2022-08-02T00:45:55+0000. See Figure 3-7 for before the execution and Figure 3-8 for after the execution.

Ansible Module vmware_guest_snapshot

- `community.vmware.vmware_guest_snapshot`

You can manage the VMware snapshots using the Ansible module `vmware_guest_snapshot`. The full name is `community.vmware.vmware_guest_snapshot`, which means it is part of the collection of modules that interact with VMware and is community supported. It manages virtual machine snapshots in vCenter.

Parameters

- hostname *string*/port *integer*/username *string*/password *string*/datacenter *string*/validate_certs *boolean*: Connection details

- state *string* - present/absent/revert/remove_all

- remove_children *boolean*: No/yes

- snapshot_name *string* description *string*: Name/description of the virtual machine to work with

- memory_dump *boolean*: No/yes because memory snapshots take time and resources

The following parameters are useful in order to take a VMware virtual machine snapshot using the module `vmware_guest_snapshot`. First, you must establish the connection with VMware vSphere or VMware vCenter using a plethora of self-explanatory parameters: `hostname`, `port`, `username`, `password`, `datacenter`, and `validate_certs`. Once the connection is successfully established, you can specify the desired snapshot state, in this case, `present` to take a snapshot. You can also `revert` or `remove` a snapshot with the same Ansible module. If you want to remove a snapshot, you can also remove all the dependent snapshots using the parameter `remove_children`. It's a good practice to set the name and description of the snapshot using the the `snapshot_name` and `description` parameters. An advanced practice is to create the memory dump of the virtual machines. Please note that memory snapshots take time and resources will take a longer time to create. By default, memory dumps are disabled but you can enable them using the `memory_dump` parameter.

Links

- community.vmware.vmware_guest_snapshot, `https://docs.ansible.com/ansible/latest/collections/community/vmware/vmware_guest_snapshot_module.html`

Code

Here's how to take a snapshot named Ansible Managed Snapshot of the virtual machine named `myvm` using an Ansible Playbook (see Figure 3-7 for before the execution and Figure 3-8 for after the execution). Let me encourage you to set a name and description to easily find it in your VMware vCenter. The Ansible Playbook includes the file `vars.yml` for common variables for the VMware infrastructure and has one task for powering one of the virtual machine with the specified name `myvm`. Under the hood, Ansible interacts with the VMware API via Python libraries to execute the operation and verify the successful startup of the virtual machine.

- vm_snapshot_create.yml

```
---
- name: vm snapshot demo
  hosts: localhost

  gather_facts: false
  collections:
    - community.vmware
  pre_tasks:
    - include_vars: vars.yml
  tasks:
    - name: create a snapshot
      vmware_guest_snapshot:
        hostname: "{{ vcenter_hostname }}"
        username: "{{ vcenter_username }}"
        password: "{{ vcenter_password }}"
        datacenter: "{{ vcenter_datacenter }}"
        validate_certs: "{{ vcenter_validate_certs }}"
        name: "{{ vm_name }}"
        state: present
        snapshot_name: "Ansible Managed Snapshot"
        folder: "{{ vm_folder }}"
        description: "This snapshot is created by Ansible Playbook"
```

The vars.yml file stores all the VMware infrastructure connection parameters that may be shared among different Ansible Playbook files.

- vars.yml

```
---
vcenter_hostname: "vmware.example.com"
vcenter_datacenter: "vmwaredatacenter"
vcenter_validate_certs: false
vcenter_username: "username@vsphere.local"
vcenter_password: "MySecretPassword123"
vm_name: "myvm"
vm_folder: "myvm"
```

The Ansible inventory is only the `localhost` because you're executing the Ansible automation on the Ansible controller.

- Inventory

  `localhost`

A successful execution output includes

- Target host: `localhost`

- Command result: `ok=2  changed=1`

- Return value:

  ```
  TASK [create snapshot]
  changed: [localhost]
  ```

You can see the result of the process of taking the VMware snapshot in the VMware virtual machine in the VMware vSphere web user interface in Figures 3-7 and 3-8.

Figure 3-7. *Before taking a VMware virtual machine snapshot with Ansible*

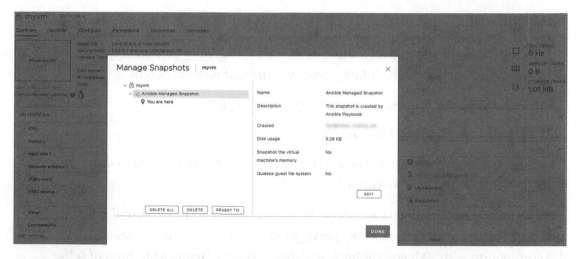

Figure 3-8. *After taking a VMware virtual machine snapshot with Ansible*

Deleting a VMware Virtual Machine Snapshot

You can automate the process of taking and removing snapshots of a VMware virtual machine by using an Ansible Playbook and the vmware_guest_snapshot module (see Figure 3-9 for before the execution and Figure 3-10 for after the execution). VMware virtual machine snapshots are a powerful way to store a particular state of a virtual machine in time, but when they start to pile up, they become difficult to manage. The higher the number of snapshots you have, the more usage of storage space is needed, so it's always a good best practice to maintain good snapshot hygiene. The traditional way of manually taking the snapshot requires access the vSphere client or web user interface. The user interface requires several interactions in order to delete one VMware snapshot. From the Ansible point of view, the vmware_guest_snapshot module identifies the virtual machine by the name myvm in this example; you can also search for a desired snapshot name, for example, Ansible Managed Snapshot.

Ansible Module vmware_guest_snapshot

- community.vmware.vmware_guest_snapshot

You can manage the VMware snapshots using the Ansible module vmware_guest_snapshot. The full name is community.vmware.vmware_guest_snapshot, which means that it is part of the collection of modules that interact with VMware and it is community supported. It manages virtual machine snapshots in vCenter.

Parameters

- hostname *string*/port *integer*/username *string*/password *string*/datacenter *string*/validate_certs *boolean*: Connection details

- state *string* - present/absent/revert/remove_all

- remove_children *boolean*: No/yes

- snapshot_name *string* description *string*: Name/description of the virtual machine to work with

The following parameters are useful in order to take a VMware virtual machine snapshot using the module vmware_guest_snapshot. First, you must establish the connection with VMware vSphere or VMware vCenter using a plethora of self-explanatory parameters: hostname, username, password, datacenter, and validate_certs. Once the connection is successfully established, you can specify the desired snapshot state, in this case, absent to delete a snapshot. You can also manage a snapshot with the same Ansible module. If you want to remove a snapshot, you can also remove all the dependent snapshots using the parameter remove_children. You need to specify the exact snapshot name that you would like to remove in the snapshot_name parameter.

Links

- community.vmware.vmware_guest_snapshot, https://docs.ansible.com/ansible/latest/collections/community/vmware/vmware_guest_snapshot_module.html

Code

I'm going to show you how to delete a snapshot named Ansible Managed Snapshot of the virtual machine named myvm using an Ansible Playbook (see Figure 3-9 for before the execution and Figure 3-10 for after the execution). The Ansible Playbook includes the file vars.yml for common variables for the VMware infrastructure and has one task for powering one of the virtual machine with the specified name myvm. Under the hood, Ansible interacts with the VMware API via Python libraries to execute the operation and verify the successful startup of the virtual machine.

- vm_snapshot_remove.yml

```
---
- name: vm snapshot demo
  hosts: localhost

  gather_facts: false
  collections:
    - community.vmware
  pre_tasks:
    - include_vars: vars.yml
  tasks:
    - name: remove snapshot
      vmware_guest_snapshot:
        hostname: "{{ vcenter_hostname }}"
        username: "{{ vcenter_username }}"
        password: "{{ vcenter_password }}"
        datacenter: "{{ vcenter_datacenter }}"
        validate_certs: "{{ vcenter_validate_certs }}"
        name: "{{ vm_name }}"
        folder: "{{ vm_folder }}"
        snapshot_name: "Ansible Managed Snapshot"
        state: absent
```

The vars.yml file stores all the VMware infrastructure connection parameters that may be shared among different Ansible Playbook files.

- vars.yml

```
---
vcenter_hostname: "vmware.example.com"
vcenter_datacenter: "vmwaredatacenter"
vcenter_validate_certs: false
vcenter_username: "username@vsphere.local"
vcenter_password: "MySecretPassword123"
vm_name: "myvm"

vm_folder: "myvm"
```

The Ansible inventory is only the `localhost` because you're executing the Ansible automation on the Ansible controller.

- Inventory

  `localhost`

A successful execution output includes

- Target host: `localhost`

- Command result: `ok=2`

- Return value:

  `TASK [remove snapshot]`
  `changed: [localhost]`

You can see the result of the delete operation for the VMware snapshot in the VMware virtual machine in the VMware vSphere web user interface in Figures 3-9 and 3-10.

Figure 3-9. *Before deleting a VMware virtual machine snapshot*

Figure 3-10. *After deleting a VMware virtual machine snapshot*

Adding a New Hard Disk to a VMware Virtual Machine

You can automate the addition of a new hard disk to a VMware virtual machine guest using an Ansible Playbook and the vmware_guest_disk module. This is useful adding extra storage to a virtual machine, one of the tedious activities for a VMware infrastructure administrator. The manual way requires you to fill out some forms and access the vSphere client or web user interface in order to add a new virtual hard drive. Please note that you should be very careful to attach the drive to the right virtual machine, one of the manual sources of the problem. A few operating systems support storage hotplugs, but most need to shut down the virtual machine before changing the storage configuration. Each virtual hard drive must be connected to a virtual storage controller. VMware supports the most used SCSI controller types (BusLogic Parallel, LSI Logic Parallel, LSI Logic SAS, and VMware Paravirtual SCSI) as well as AHCI, SATA, and the newest releases, plus NVM Express (NVMe) controllers. Check the maximum number of supported virtual storage controllers in your running VMware infrastructure version (maximum of four SCSI controllers and four SATA controllers) in the latest releases. Let's see how to automate the addition of a 1GB hard disk to a VMware virtual machine guest named myvm using an Ansible Playbook and vmware_guest_disk module (see Figure 3-11 for before the execution and Figure 3-12 for after the execution). This operation only adds the virtual hard drive; you should partition and format a filesystem via the operating system. This operation varies operating system by operating system: Linux uses CLI and GUI `fdisk`, `parted`, `gparted`, `qtparted`, `KDE Partition Manager` and `GNOME Disks Utility`, macOS uses `Disk Utility`, and Windows uses `Disk Management`.

Ansible Module vmware_guest_disk

- `community.vmware.vmware_guest_disk`

You can manage VMware virtual hard drives using the Ansible module `vmware_guest_disk`. The full name is `community.vmware.vmware_guest_disk`, which means that it is part of the collection of modules that interact with VMware and is community supported. It manages disks related to the virtual machines in a given vCenter infrastructure.

Parameters

- hostname *string*/port *integer*/username *string*/password *string*/datacenter *string*/validate_certs *boolean*: Connection details

- datacenter *string*: The datacenter name to which the virtual machine belongs to

- scsi_controller/unit_number/scsi_type *string*: SCSI controller details

- size/size_kb/size_mb/size_gb/size_tb *string*: Disk storage size

- disk_mode *string* — persistent/independent_persistent/independent_nonpersistent

The following parameters are useful in order to add a disk to VMware virtual machine using the module `vmware_guest_disk`. First, you must establish the connection with VMware vSphere or VMware vCenter using a plethora of self-explanatory parameters: `hostname`, `username`, `password`, `datacenter`, and `validate_certs`.

Once the connection is successfully established, you can specify the desired disk configuration: in this case, it's to add a new disk to the virtual machine. The mandatory parameters are only `datacenter` and `unit_number`.

The `datacenter` parameter specifies which datacenter name the virtual machine belongs to, for resource allocations.

The disk must be connected to a SCSI controller inside the virtual machine, so you should specify all the small details like `scsi_controller`, `unit_number`, and `scsi_type`.

According to SCSI standards, valid SCSI controller numbers are from 0 to 29, and unit numbers are from 0 to 15.

You may be interested in taking a deep dive into performance analysis to properly adjust these parameters.

You can specify the disk size via various parameters according to the needed size unit: kb, MB, GB, TB, etc.

One of the most important parameters is the disk_mode (defaults to persistent mode). Other options are independent_persistent and independent_nonpersistent.

Links

- community.vmware.vmware_guest_disk, https://docs.ansible. com/ansible/latest/collections/community/vmware/vmware_ guest_disk_module.html

Code

I'm going to show you how to add a 1GB disk to a virtual machine named myvm using an Ansible Playbook in the SCSI controller number 1 and unit number 1 (see Figure 3-11 for before the execution and Figure 3-12 for after the execution). The Ansible Playbook includes the file vars.yml for some common variables for the VMware infrastructure and has one task for adding a disk to the virtual machine with the specified name myvm. Under the hood, Ansible interacts with VMware API via Python libraries to execute the operation and verify the successful startup of the virtual machine.

- vm_add_disk.yml

```
---

- name: vm disk demo
  hosts: localhost

  gather_facts: false
  collections:
    - community.vmware
  pre_tasks:
    - include_vars: vars.yml
  tasks:
    - name: add disk to vm
```

```
                    vmware_guest_disk:
                      hostname: "{{ vcenter_hostname }}"
                      username: "{{ vcenter_username }}"
                      password: "{{ vcenter_password }}"
                      validate_certs: "{{ vcenter_validate_certs }}"
                      datacenter: "{{ vcenter_datacenter }}"
                      name: "{{ vm_name }}"
                      disk:
                        - size_gb: "{{ vm_disk_gb }}"
                          type: "{{ vm_disk_type }}"
                          datastore: "{{ vm_disk_datastore }}"
                          state: present
                          scsi_controller: "{{ vm_disk_scsi_controller }}"
                          unit_number: "{{ vm_disk_scsi_unit }}"
                          scsi_type: "{{ vm_disk_scsi_type }}"
                          disk_mode: "{{ vm_disk_mode }}"
```

The vars.yml file stores all the VMware infrastructure connection parameters that may be shared among different Ansible Playbook files.

- vars.yml

```
---
vcenter_hostname: "vmware.example.com"
vcenter_datacenter: "vmwaredatacenter"
vcenter_validate_certs: false
vcenter_username: "username@vsphere.local"
vcenter_password: "MySecretPassword123"
vm_name: "myvm"
vm_disk_gb: 1
vm_disk_type: "thin"
vm_disk_datastore: "datastore"
vm_disk_scsi_controller: 1
vm_disk_scsi_unit: 1
vm_disk_scsi_type: 'paravirtual'
vm_disk_mode: 'persistent'
```

The Ansible inventory is only the `localhost` because you're executing the Ansible automation on the Ansible controller.

- Inventory

  `localhost`

A successful execution output includes

- Target host: `localhost`

- Command result: `ok=2 changed=1`

- Return value:

  ```
  TASK [add disk to vm]
  changed: [localhost]
  ```

You can see the result of the addition of the virtual disk in the VMware virtual machine in the VMware vSphere web user interface in Figures 3-11 and 3-12.

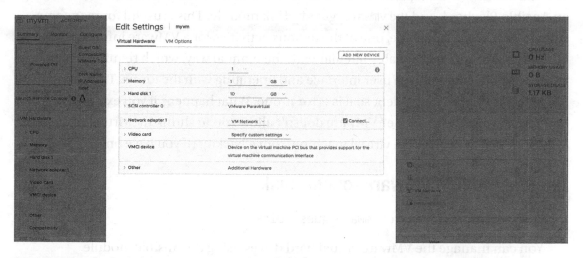

Figure 3-11. *Before adding a new hard disk to a VMware virtual machine*

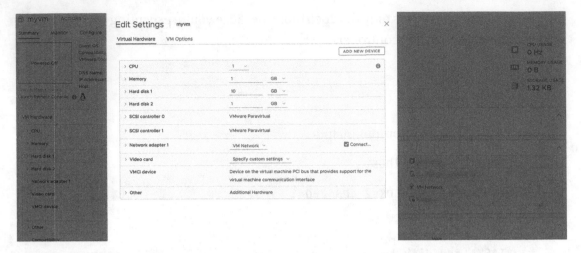

Figure 3-12. *After adding a new hard disk to a VMware virtual machine*

Expanding a Virtual Disk in a VMware Virtual Machine

You can automate the expansion of a hard disk to a VMware virtual machine guest using an Ansible Playbook and the vmware_guest_disk module. This is useful for managing storage on a virtual machine, one of the tedious activities for a VMware infrastructure administrator. You are probably familiar with the manual way, which requires access to the vSphere client or web user interface and operating with the forms. This manual operation is human dependent so it is error prone. What happens if you extend the space to the wrong virtual machine? VMware doesn't allow you to shrink the virtual disk, so the only option is to recover the virtual machine from a backup (if you have one).

Ansible Module vmware_guest_disk

- community.vmware.vmware_guest_disk

You can manage the VMware virtual hard drives using the Ansible module vmware_guest_disk. The full name is community.vmware.vmware_guest_disk, which means that it is part of the collection of modules that interact with VMware and is community supported. It manages disks related to a virtual machine in a given vCenter infrastructure.

Parameters

- hostname *string*/port *integer*/username *string*/password *string*/ datacenter *string*/validate_certs *boolean*: Connection details

- datacenter *string*: The datacenter name to which the virtual machine belongs to

- scsi_controller/unit_number/scsi_type *string*: SCSI controller details

- size/size_kb/size_mb/size_gb/size_tb *string*: Disk storage size

- disk_mode *string* — persistent/independent_persistent/ independent_nonpersistent

The following parameters are useful in order to expand a virtual disk in a VMware virtual machine using the module vmware_guest_disk. First, you must establish the connection with VMware vSphere or VMware vCenter using a plethora of self-explanatory parameters: hostname, username, password, datacenter, and validate_ certs. Once the connection is successfully established, you can specify the desired disk configuration. In this expansion, a disk is connected to a virtual machine. The mandatory parameters are only datacenter and unit_number. The datacenter parameter specifies which datacenter name the virtual machine belongs to, for resource allocations. The disk must be connected to a SCSI controller inside the virtual machine, so you should specify all the small details like scsi_controller, unit_number, and scsi_type. According to SCSI standards, valid SCSI controller numbers are from 0 to 29, and unit numbers are from 0 to 15. You may be interested in a deep dive into some performance analysis to properly adjust these parameters. You can specify the disk size via various parameters according to the needed size unit: kb, MB, GB, TB, etc. One of the most important parameters is the disk_mode (defaults to persistent mode). Other options are independent_persistent and independent_nonpersistent.

Links

- community.vmware.vmware_guest_disk, https://docs.ansible. com/ansible/latest/collections/community/vmware/vmware_ guest_disk_module.html

Code

I'm going to show you how to expand the size of an additional disk connected to a virtual machine named myvm using an Ansible Playbook. The disk is connected to SCSI controller number 1 and has unit number 1 (see Figure 3-13 for before the execution and Figure 3-14 for after the execution). The virtual hard disk had a size of 1GB and you want to expand it to 2GB. The Ansible Playbook includes the file vars.yml for common variables for the VMware infrastructure and has one task for expanding the virtual hard disk of the virtual machine with the specified name myvm. Under the hood, Ansible interacts with the VMware API via Python libraries to execute the operation and verify the successful startup of the virtual machine.

- vm_disk_expand.yml

```
---
- name: vm disk demo
  hosts: localhost

  gather_facts: false
  collections:
    - community.vmware
  pre_tasks:
    - include_vars: vars.yml
  tasks:
    - name: expand disk in vm
      vmware_guest_disk:
        hostname: "{{ vcenter_hostname }}"
        username: "{{ vcenter_username }}"
        password: "{{ vcenter_password }}"
        validate_certs: "{{ vcenter_validate_certs }}"
        datacenter: "{{ vcenter_datacenter }}"
        name: "{{ vm_name }}"
        disk:
          - size_gb: "{{ vm_disk_gb }}"
            type: "{{ vm_disk_type }}"
            datastore: "{{ vm_disk_datastore }}"
            state: present
```

```
                scsi_controller: "{{ vm_disk_scsi_controller }}"
                unit_number: "{{ vm_disk_scsi_unit }}"
                scsi_type: "{{ vm_disk_scsi_type }}"
                disk_mode: "{{ vm_disk_mode }}"
```

The vars.yml file stores all the VMware infrastructure connection parameters that may be shared among different Ansible Playbook files.

- vars.yml

```
---
vcenter_hostname: "vmware.example.com"
vcenter_datacenter: "vmwaredatacenter"
vcenter_validate_certs: false
vcenter_username: "username@vsphere.local"
vcenter_password: "MySecretPassword123"
vm_name: "myvm"
vm_disk_gb: 2
vm_disk_type: "thin"
vm_disk_datastore: "datastore"
vm_disk_scsi_controller: 1
vm_disk_scsi_unit: 1
vm_disk_scsi_type: 'paravirtual'
vm_disk_mode: 'persistent'
```

The Ansible inventory is only the localhost because you're executing the Ansible automation on the Ansible controller.

- Inventory

  localhost

A successful execution output includes

- Target host: localhost

- Command result: ok=2 changed=1

- Return value:

```
TASK [expand disk in vm]
changed: [localhost]
```

You can see the result of the expansion of the virtual disk in the VMware virtual machine in the VMware vSphere web user interface in Figures 3-13 and 3-14.

Figure 3-13. *Before expanding a virtual disk in a VMware virtual machine*

Figure 3-14. *After expanding a virtual disk in a VMware virtual machine*

Gathering VMware Host Information on a Cluster

You can automate the information gathering of VMware ESX/ESXi hosts in a VMware cluster using an Ansible Playbook and the `vmware_host_config_info` module. Reporting is a good management practice that every VMware infrastructure administrator usually performs on a regular basis. Reporting enables resource planning, allocation, and optimization aligned to the business needs. You are probably used to performing this task manually by accessing the vSphere client or web user interface and navigating through the various forms for each cluster and VMware ESX/ESXi host. This is exactly the repetitive and boring kind of task that automation can simplify to prevent errors and save time.

Ansible Module vmware_host_config_info

- `community.vmware.vmware_host_config_info`

You can collect configuration and runtime information about a VMware ESXi host using the Ansible module `vmware_host_config_info`. The full name is `community.vmware.vmware_host_config_info`, which means that it is part of the collection of modules that interact with VMware and is community supported. The module's purpose is to gather an ESXi host's advanced configuration information.

Parameters

- hostname *string*/port *integer*/username *string*/password *string*/ datacenter *string*/validate_certs *boolean*: Connection details

- cluster_name *string*: Name of the cluster to which the ESXi host belongs

- esxi_hostname *string*: ESXi hostname to gather information from.

The following parameters are useful in order to gather information about all VMware ESX/ESXi hosts in the given cluster using the module `vmware_host_config_info`. First, you must establish the connection with VMware vSphere or VMware vCenter using a plethora of self-explanatory parameters: `hostname`, `port`, `username`, `password`, `datacenter`, and `validate_certs`.

Once the connection is successfully established, you can specify the full `esxi_hostname`, the ESX/ESXi hostname, or list all the hostnames in the current cluster `cluster_name`.

Links

- `community.vmware.vmware_host_config_info`, https://docs. ansible.com/ansible/latest/collections/community/vmware/ vmware_cluster_info_module.html

Code

I'm going to show you how to gather configuration information on all the ESX/ESXi hosts in the current VMware `production` cluster using an Ansible Playbook. The Ansible Playbook includes the file `vars.yml` for some common variables for the VMware infrastructure and has two tasks. The first task acquires information from the VMware `production` cluster and saves the result in the `cluster_info` Ansible variable. The second task prints onscreen the values of the `cluster_info` Ansible variable. In a real-world scenario, you can also perform operations based on the status of the `cluster_info` Ansible variable. Under the hood, Ansible interacts with the VMware API via Python libraries to execute the operation and verify the successful startup of the virtual machine.

- `host_info_cluser.yml`

```
---
- name: host in cluster info demo
  hosts: localhost

  gather_facts: false
  collections:
    - community.vmware
  pre_tasks:
    - include_vars: vars.yml
  tasks:
    - name: Gather info about all ESXi Host in the given Cluster
      community.vmware.vmware_host_config_info:
        hostname: '{{ vcenter_hostname }}'
```

```
            username: '{{ vcenter_username }}'
            password: '{{ vcenter_password }}'
            validate_certs: "{{ vcenter_validate_certs }}"
            cluster_name: "{{ cluster_name }}"
        register: cluster_info

      - name: print cluster info
        ansible.builtin.debug:
          var: cluster_info
```

The vars.yml file stores all the VMware infrastructure connection parameters that may be shared among different Ansible Playbook files.

- vars.yml

```
---
vcenter_hostname: "vmware.example.com"
vcenter_datacenter: "vmwaredatacenter"
vcenter_validate_certs: false
vcenter_username: "username@vsphere.local"
vcenter_password: "MySecretPassword123"
cluster_name: "production"
```

The Ansible inventory is only the localhost because you're executing the Ansible automation on the Ansible controller.

- Inventory

```
localhost
```

A successful execution output includes

- Target host: localhost

- Command result: ok=3 changed=0

- Return value:

```
TASK [Gather info about all ESXi Host in the given Cluster]
ok: [localhost]
TASK [print cluster info]
```

131

```
ok: [localhost] => {
    "cluster_info": {
        "changed": false,
        "failed": false,
        "hosts_info": {
            "esxi1.example.com": {
                "Annotations.WelcomeMessage": "",
                "BufferCache.FlushInterval": 30000,
[...]
                "Vpx.Vpxa.config.workingDir": "/var/log/
                vmware/vpx",
                "XvMotion.VMFSOptimizations": 1
            }
        }
    }
}
```

Getting a VMware Virtual Machine UUID

You can automate the gathering of the UUID of a VMware virtual machine using
an Ansible Playbook and the vmware_guest_info module. The Universally Unique
Identifier (UUID) identifies in a unique way the virtual machine in your VMware
infrastructure. It's created the first time you power on the virtual machine. It's extremely
useful for performing day-to-day operations as well as the VMware motion between
hosts. It's better than a virtual machine name because it uniquely identifies the virtual
machine. The drawback is that it is composed of a 128-bit integer, so it's not the best
mnemonical value! It's usually printed in the hex value with dashes.

Ansible Module vmware_guest_info

- community.vmware.vmware_guest_info

You can collect information about a VMware virtual machine using the Ansible
module vmware_guest_info. The full name is community.vmware.vmware_guest_info,
which means that it is part of the collection of modules that interact with VMware and

it's community supported. The module's purpose is to gather info about a single VM. The `vmware_guest_info` module is a substitute for the previous deprecated `community.vmware.vmware_guest_facts` module that will be removed in a major release after 2021-12-01.

Parameters

- hostname *string*/port *integer*/username *string*/password *string*/datacenter *string*/validate_certs *boolean*: Connection details

- name *string*: Virtual machine name

The following parameters are useful in order to Get VMware vSphere virtual machine UUID using the module `vmware_guest_info`. First, you must establish the connection with VMware vSphere or VMware vCenter using a plethora of self-explanatory parameters: `hostname`, `port`, `username`, `password`, `datacenter`, and `validate_certs`. Once the connection is successfully established, you can specify the virtual machine name to obtain all information about it.

Links

- `community.vmware.vmware_guest_info`, https://docs.ansible. com/ansible/latest/collections/community/vmware/vmware_ guest_info_module.html

Code

I'm going to show you how to gather information about a specific `myvm` VMware virtual machine and select the UUID using an Ansible Playbook (see Figure 3-15). The Ansible Playbook includes the file `vars.yml` for common variables for the VMware Infrastructure and has two tasks. The first task acquires information from the `myvm` VMware virtual machine and saves the result in the `detailed_vm_info` Ansible variable. The second task prints onscreen the values of the `detailed_vm_info` Ansible variable. Specifically, the UUID value is stored inside the `detailed_vm_info.instance.hw_product_uuid` parameter. Under the hood, Ansible interacts with the VMware API via Python libraries to execute the operation and verify the successful startup of the virtual machine.

- vm_uuid.yml

```
---
- name: vm UUID demo
  hosts: localhost

  gather_facts: false
  collections:
    - community.vmware
  pre_tasks:
    - include_vars: vars.yml
  tasks:
    - name: Get VM UUID
      vmware_guest_info:
        hostname: "{{ vcenter_hostname }}"
        username: "{{ vcenter_username }}"
        password: "{{ vcenter_password }}"
        datacenter: "{{ vcenter_datacenter }}"
        validate_certs: "{{ vcenter_validate_certs }}"
        name: "{{ vm_name }}"
      register: detailed_vm_info
    - name: print VM UUID
      ansible.builtin.debug:
        var: detailed_vm_info.instance.hw_product_uuid
```

The vars.yml file stores all the VMware infrastructure connection parameters that may be shared among different Ansible Playbook files.

- vars.yml

```
---
vcenter_hostname: "vmware.example.com"
vcenter_datacenter: "vmwaredatacenter"
vcenter_validate_certs: false
vcenter_username: "username@vsphere.local"
vcenter_password: "MySecretPassword123"
vm_name: "myvm"
```

The Ansible inventory is only the localhost because you're executing the Ansible automation on the Ansible controller.

- Inventory

localhost

A successful execution output includes

- Target host: localhost

- Command result: ok=3 changed=0

- Return value:

```
TASK [Get VM UUID]
ok: [localhost]
TASK [print VM UUID]
ok: [localhost] => {
    "detailed_vm_info.instance.hw_product_uuid": "4225a846-
    b176-892d-0e27-10a4106269a0"
}
```

You can see the result of gathering the UUID of a VMware virtual machine in the VMware vSphere web user interface. You can find this information in the VMware vSphere web console under "Hosts and Clusters" or "VMs and Templates." The list view shows a lot of information such as state, status, provisioned and used space, host CPU, and memory. If the list doesn't show the UUID columns, click the gray area of one column and select Show/Hide Columns and enable UUID from the pop-up list. See Figure 3-15.

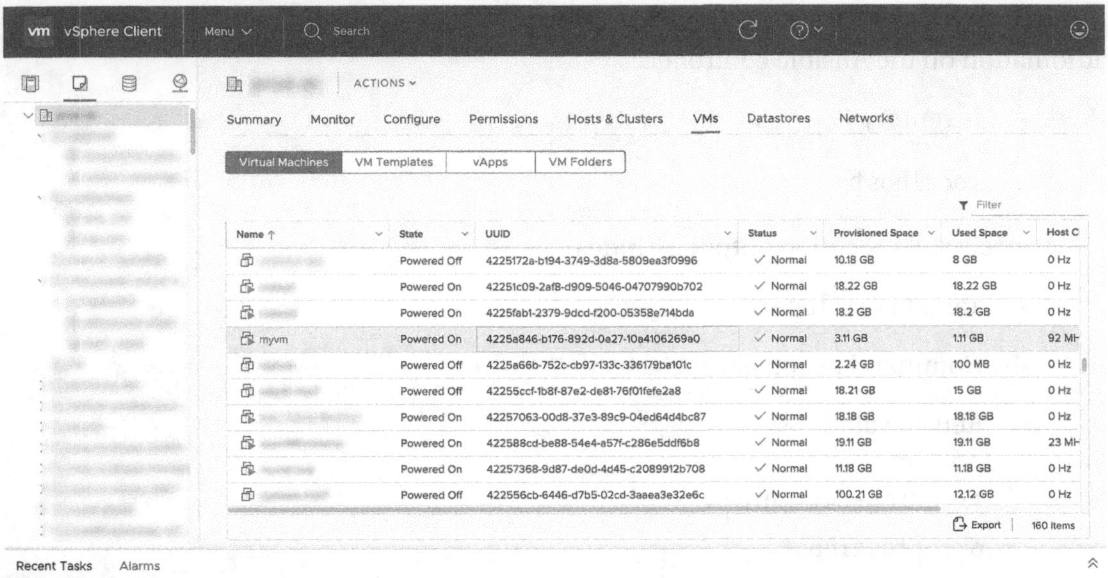

Figure 3-15. *vmware_guest_info after execution*

Ansible Dynamic Inventory For VMware

You can automate listing the virtual machines in your VMware infrastructure using the
vmware_vm_inventory Ansible Inventory plugin. One of the advantages of this plugin
is that you can use the dynamic listing as an Ansible inventory for your execution.
Inventory plugins allow you to expand the capabilities of your Ansible by creating
a listing of the target nodes on the fly from a specified data source. The data source
contains the connection parameter to your VMware infrastructure and the output
contains the list of all the virtual machines. There is no manual way to accomplish this
task except to manually create an Ansible inventory of VMware virtual machines. The
manual creation of the Ansible inventory is error prone by nature because even a simple
typo can have a huge impact on an execution, such as a failure or wrong target host.

Ansible vmware_vm_inventory

- `community.vmware.vmware_vm_inventory`

The Ansible Inventory Plugin queries your VMware infrastructure via the VMware
APIs and returns to Ansible a list of virtual machines that can be used as target nodes.
The purpose is to get virtual machines as inventory hosts from the VMware environment.
In this way, you can execute your Ansible automation to all your virtual machines,

for example. Please note that the inventory YAML configuration file MUST end with `vmware.yml`, `vmware.yaml`, `vmware_vm_inventory.yml`, or `vmware_vm_inventory.yaml` file names. The full name is `community.vmware.vmware_vm_inventory`, which means that it is part of the collection of modules that interact with VMware and is community supported.

- Python requirements

As with the `community.vmware` collection, this plugin requires the `pyVmomi` Python library installed in your Ansible controller. For advanced parameters such as the tag feature, you must install the VMware vSphere Automation SDK for Python library.

Links

- `community.vmware.vmware_vm_inventory`, https://docs.ansible. com/ansible/latest/collections/community/vmware/vmware_vm_ inventory_inventory.html

Code

In this example, you are going to list all the available virtual machines and specifically the `myvm` test machine created earlier in this book.

The first step is to specifically enable the `vmware_vm_inventory` Ansible Inventory Plugin in your configuration file. You can enable it via `ansible.cfg` in the current path or system-wide via /etc/ansible/ansible.cfg. Simply add the `vmware_vm_inventory` plugin name inside the key `enable_plugins` in the `inventory` section.

- `ansible.cfg`

```
[inventory]
enable_plugins = vmware_vm_inventory
```

The second step is to create the data source with your VMware infrastructure connection parameters. The following is a simple YAML data source to list all the virtual machines that connect to `vmware.example.com` VMware vSphere with a given username and password and to disable the SSL certificate validation (for self-signed certificates). It enables group mapping of the results by VMware virtual machines. It disables tags associated with the VMware virtual machines (requires vSphere Automation SDK Python library).

- inventory.vmware.yml

```
plugin: vmware_vm_inventory
strict: False
hostname: vmware.example.com
username: username@vsphere.local
password: MySecretPassword123
validate_certs: False
with_tags: False
groups:
  VMs: True
```

The default view output shows all the available VMware properties associated with the VMware virtual machine. Specifying the properties parameter in the YAML data source, you can display only the ones needed, such as name, config. cpuHotAddEnabled, config.cpuHotRemoveEnabled, config.instanceUuid, config. hardware.numCPU, config.template, config.name, config.uuid, guest.hostName, guest.ipAddress, guest.guestId, guest.guestState, runtime.maxMemoryUsage, customValue, summary.runtime.powerState, and config.guestId. Here is an example of the properties parameter to display only the power state and the name of the virtual machine:

```
properties:
  - 'runtime.powerState'
  - 'config.name'
```

Another useful parameter is filters, which allows you to search only for virtual machines in a particular state. Here is an example of the filters parameter to search only the virtual machine in a powered-on state:

```
filters:
  - runtime.powerState == "poweredOn"
```

Here is an example of the filters parameter to search only for the virtual machine with a specific operating system class:

```
filters:
  - config.guestId == "rhel7_64Guest"
```

The `ansible-inventory` tool can generate a JSON list view using the inventory data source `inventory.vmware.yml` as input.

```
$ ansible-inventory -i inventory.vmware.yml --list
```

A successful execution output includes the following output for the `myvm` VMware virtual machine:

```
$ ansible-inventory -i inventory.vmware.yml --list
{
    "VMs": {
        "hosts": [
            "myvm_42254893-3793-0e4f-9f61-7c37d244c2a8"
        ]
    },
    "_meta": {
        "hostvars": {
            "myvm_42254893-3793-0e4f-9f61-7c37d244c2a8": {
                "config": {
                    "cpuHotAddEnabled": false,
                    "cpuHotRemoveEnabled": false,
                    "guestId": "centos64Guest",
                    "hardware": {
                        "numCPU": 1
                    },
                    "instanceUuid": "5025d3e9-6c26-30b5-d29a-2c1be5fa3862",
                    "name": "myvm",
                    "template": false,
                    "uuid": "42254893-3793-0e4f-9f61-7c37d244c2a8"
                },
                "config.cpuHotAddEnabled": false,
                "config.cpuHotRemoveEnabled": false,
                "config.guestId": "centos64Guest",
                "config.hardware.numCPU": 1,
                "config.instanceUuid": "5025d3e9-6c26-30b5-
                d29a-2c1be5fa3862",
                "config.name": "myvm",
```

```
            "config.template": false,
            "config.uuid": "42254893-3793-0e4f-9f61-7c37d244c2a8",
            "guest": {
                "guestState": "notRunning"
            },
            "guest.guestState": "notRunning",
            "name": "myvm",
            "runtime": {
                "connectionState": "connected"
            },
            "runtime.connectionState": "connected",
            "summary": {
                "runtime": {
                    "powerState": "poweredOff"
                }
            },
            "summary.runtime.powerState": "poweredOff"
        }
    }
},
"all": {
    "children": [
        "VMs",
        "centos64Guest",
        "poweredOff",
        "ungrouped"
    ]
},
"VMs": {
    "hosts": [
        "myvm_42254893-3793-0e4f-9f61-7c37d244c2a8"
    ]
},
```

```
    "centos64Guest": {
        "hosts": [
            "myvm_42254893-3793-0e4f-9f61-7c37d244c2a8"
        ]
    },
    "poweredOff": {
        "hosts": [
            "myvm_42254893-3793-0e4f-9f61-7c37d244c2a8"
        ]
    }
}
```

The `ansible-inventory` tool can also generate a graph view using the inventory data source `inventory.vmware.yml` as input. This view is useful to visualize the relationship with other VMware infrastructure resources.

```
$ ansible-inventory -i inventory.vmware.yml --graph
```

A successful execution output includes all the groups related to the `myvm` VMware virtual machine:

```
@all:
  |--@VMs:
  |  |--myvm_42254893-3793-0e4f-9f61-7c37d244c2a8
  |--@centos64Guest:
  |  |--myvm_42254893-3793-0e4f-9f61-7c37d244c2a8
  |--@poweredOff:
  |  |--myvm_42254893-3793-0e4f-9f61-7c37d244c2a8
```

You can use the groups as a source for an Ansible Playbook execution. In this way, you obtain the execution of your Ansible Playbook across all the dynamically generated Ansible inventories. In the previous example, the `myvm` machine is part of the `all`, `VMs`, `centos64Guest`, and `poweredOff` groups.

Now you can use your Ansible dynamic inventory for VMware in any Ansible interaction such as the ad-hoc `ping` command against the `all` target nodes group.

```
$ ansible -i inventory.vmware.yml all -m ping
```

The best result can be obtained by combining Ansible dynamic inventory for VMware and an Ansible Playbook using the `ansible-playbook` command.

```
$ ansible-playbook -i inventory.vmware.yml playbook.yml
```

In this way, you're able to execute the Ansible Playbook named `playbook.yml` against the dynamically generated list of all the virtual machines in your VMware infrastructure.

Getting a VMware Virtual Machine Running Host

You can automate the gathering of the running host of a VMware virtual machine using an Ansible Playbook and the `vmware_guest_info` module (see Figure 3-16). Refer to the "Getting a VMware Virtual Machine UUID" section for more details about the `vmware_guest_info` module. Accessing the current running host of the VMware virtual machine is useful to produce an accurate report of the infrastructure's current load distribution, to better distribute the workload between VMware host resources, and to perform the day-to-day operations as well as the VMware motion between hosts.

Code

I'm going to show you how to gather information about the `myvm` VMware virtual machine and select the running host using an Ansible Playbook. The Ansible Playbook includes the file **vars.yml** for some common variables for the VMware infrastructure and has two tasks. The first task acquires information from the `myvm` VMware virtual machine and saves the result in the `detailed_vm_info` Ansible variable. The second task prints onscreen the values of the `detailed_vm_info` Ansible variable. Specifically, the running host value is stored inside the `detailed_vm_info.instance.hw_esxi_host` return value. Under the hood, Ansible interacts with the VMware API via Python libraries to execute the operation and verify the successful startup of the virtual machine.

- `vm_running_host.yml`

```
---
- name: vm running host demo
  hosts: localhost

  gather_facts: false
  collections:
```

```
        - community.vmware
    pre_tasks:
      - include_vars: vars.yml
    tasks:
      - name: Get VM info
        vmware_guest_info:
          hostname: "{{ vcenter_hostname }}"
          username: "{{ vcenter_username }}"
          password: "{{ vcenter_password }}"
          datacenter: "{{ vcenter_datacenter }}"
          validate_certs: "{{ vcenter_validate_certs }}"
          name: "{{ vm_name }}"
        register: detailed_vm_info

      - name: print VM Running Host
        ansible.builtin.debug:
          var: detailed_vm_info.instance.hw_esxi_host
```

The `vars.yml` file stores all the VMware infrastructure connection parameters that may be shared among different Ansible Playbook files.

- `vars.yml`

```
    ---
    vcenter_hostname: "vmware.example.com"
    vcenter_datacenter: "vmwaredatacenter"
    vcenter_validate_certs: false
    vcenter_username: "username@vsphere.local"
    vcenter_password: "MySecretPassword123"
    vm_name: "myvm"
```

The Ansible inventory is only the `localhost` because you're executing the Ansible automation on the Ansible controller.

- Inventory

```
    localhost
```

A successful execution output includes

- Target host: `localhost`

- Command result: `ok=3 changed=0`

- Return value:

```
TASK [print VM Running Host]
ok: [localhost] => {
    "detailed_vm_info.instance.hw_esxi_host": "host1.vmware.
    example"
}
```

The execution of this code is idempotent.

You can see the result of the gathering of the running host of a VMware virtual machine in the VMware vSphere web user interface in the "host" field on the Summary page in Figure 3-16.

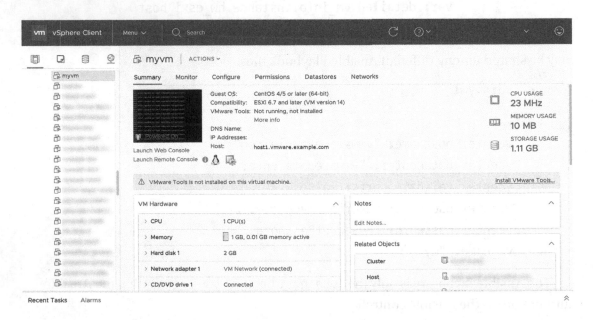

Figure 3-16. *Getting a VMware virtual machine running host via the VMware vSphere web UI*

Getting VMware Datastore Status

You can automate the gathering of the status of a VMware vSphere datastore using an Ansible Playbook and the `vmware_datastore_info` module (see Figure 3-17). Datastores in VMware vSphere are storage resources for virtual machines and VMware resource that use the VMFS file systems. VMware infrastructure administrators know that storage plays a key role in a healthy and performance infrastructure. An accurate report of the current capacity, provisioned, free space, and maintenance mode information of the VMware datastore is crucial for a better distribution of the workload between VMware resources and it's useful for performing day-to-day operations as well as the VMware storage motion.

Ansible Module vmware_datastore_info

- `community.vmware.vmware_datastore_info`

You can collect information about a VMware datastore using the Ansible module `vmware_datastore_info`. The full name is `community.vmware.vmware_datastore_info`, which means that it is part of the collection of modules that interact with VMware and is community supported. The module's purpose is to gather information about datastores available in a specific VMware vCenter.

Parameters

- hostname *string*/port *integer*/username *string*/password *string*/ datacenter *string*/validate_certs *boolean*: Connection details

- name *string*: Datastore name

The following parameters are useful in order to get the VMware vSphere datastore status using the module `vmware_datastore_info`. First, you must establish the connection with VMware vSphere or VMware vCenter using a plethora of self-explanatory parameters: `hostname`, `port`, `username`, `password`, `datacenter`, and `validate_certs`. Once the connection is successfully established, you can specify the datastore `name` to obtain all information about it.

Links

- community.vmware.vmware_datastore_info, https://docs.
  ansible.com/ansible/latest/collections/community/vmware/
  vmware_datastore_info_module.html

Code

I'm going to show you how to gather information about a specific VMware vSphere datastore using an Ansible Playbook (see Figure 3-17). The Ansible Playbook includes the file vars.yml for some common variables for the VMware infrastructure and has two tasks. The first task acquires information from the Datastore VMware vSphere datastore and saves the result in the datastore_info Ansible variable. The second task prints onscreen the values of the datastore_info Ansible variable. Under the hood, Ansible interacts with the VMware API via Python libraries to execute the operation and verify the successful startup of the virtual machine.

- datastore_info.yml

```
---
- name: datastore info demo
  hosts: localhost

  gather_facts: false
  collections:
    - community.vmware
  pre_tasks:
    - include_vars: vars.yml
  tasks:
    - name: datastore info
      vmware_datastore_info:
        hostname: "{{ vcenter_hostname }}"
        username: "{{ vcenter_username }}"
        password: "{{ vcenter_password }}"
        validate_certs: "{{ vcenter_validate_certs }}"
        datacenter_name: "{{ vcenter_datacenter }}"
        name: "{{ vcenter_datastore }}"
      register: datastore_info
```

```
    - name: print datastore info
      ansible.builtin.debug:
        var: datastore_info
```

The vars.yml file stores all the VMware infrastructure connection parameters that may be shared among different Ansible Playbook files.

- vars.yml

```
---

vcenter_hostname: "vmware.example.com"
vcenter_datacenter: "vmwaredatacenter"
vcenter_validate_certs: false
vcenter_username: "username@vsphere.local"
vcenter_password: "MySecretPassword123"
vcenter_datastore: "Datastore"
```

The Ansible inventory is only the localhost because you're executing the Ansible automation on the Ansible controller.

- Inventory

```
localhost
```

A successful execution output includes

- Target host: localhost

- Command result: ok=3 changed=0

- Return value:

```
TASK [datastore info]
ok: [localhost]
TASK [print datastore info]
ok: [localhost] => {
    "datastore_info": {
        "changed": false,
        "datastores": [
            {
                "accessible": true,
```

```
                "capacity": 3298266447872,
                "datastore_cluster": "N/A",
                "freeSpace": 26407337984,
                "maintenanceMode": "normal",
                "multipleHostAccess": true,
                "name": "Datastore",
                "provisioned": 4256761358544,
                "type": "VMFS",
                "uncommitted": 984902248656,
                "url": "ds:///vmfs/volumes/57a8979d-
                e0af2c70-3730-141877595c4b/"
            }
        ],
        "failed": false
    }
}
```

You can see the result of the gathering of the VMware vSphere datastore status and information in the VMware vSphere web user interface in Figure 3-17. You can find this information in the VMware vSphere web console, in the "Storage" area.

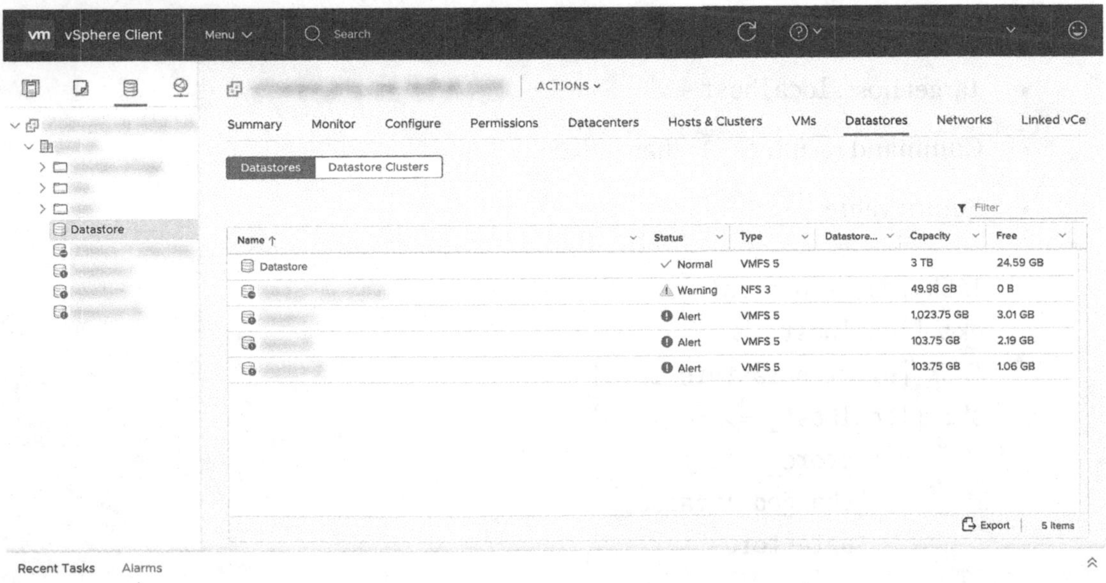

Figure 3-17. *Getting VMware datastore status in the VMware vSphere web UI*

Uploading a File to the VMware Datastore

You can automate the uploading of a file in the VMware vSphere datastore using an Ansible Playbook and the `vsphere_copy` module (see Figure 3-18 for before the execution and Figure 3-19 for after the execution). The VMware datastore is the VMware storage area where virtual machines and VMware resources are shared between VMware hosts. The VMware infrastructure administrator uploads ISO image files before creating a new VMware virtual machine.

Ansible Module vsphere_copy

- `community.vmware.vsphere_copy`

You can collect information about a VMware datastore using the Ansible module `vsphere_copy`. The full name is `community.vmware.vsphere_copy`, which means that it is part of the collection of modules that interact with VMware and is community supported. The module's purpose is to copy a file to a VMware vSphere datastore.

Parameters

- hostname *string*/port *integer*/username *string*/password *string*/ datacenter *string*/validate_certs *boolean*: Connection details

- datastore *string*: Datastore name

- src *string*: Source file name

- path *string*: Destination file name

The following parameters are useful in order to copy a file to a VMware vSphere datastore status using the module `vsphere_copy`. First, you must establish the connection with VMware vSphere or VMware vCenter using a plethora of self-explanatory parameters: `hostname`, `port`, `username`, `password`, `datacenter`, and `validate_certs`. Once the connection is successfully established, you can specify the source `src` file in the Ansible controller filesystem, the target VMware datastore `datastore`, and the target `path` datastore filename.

Links

- community.vmware.vsphere_copy, https://docs.ansible.com/
  ansible/latest/collections/community/vmware/vsphere_copy_
  module.html

Code

I'm going to show you how to upload the file ubuntu-22.04-live-server-amd64.iso
ISO image to the Datastore VMware vSphere datastore using an Ansible Playbook.
The source and destination paths are specified as variables mysrc and mydest, and you
can customize them in the Ansible Playbook or use as extra variables via the command
line. The Ansible Playbook includes the file vars.yml for some common variables for
the VMware infrastructure and has one task. Under the hood, Ansible interacts with
the VMware API via Python libraries to execute the operation and verify the successful
startup of the virtual machine.

- datastore_info.yml

```
---
- name: datastore copy demo
  hosts: localhost

  gather_facts: false
  vars:
    mysrc: "iso/ubuntu-22.04-live-server-amd64.iso"
    mydest: "ISO/ubuntu-22.04-live-server-amd64.iso"
  collections:
    - community.vmware
  pre_tasks:
    - include_vars: vars.yml
  tasks:
    - name: copy file to datastore
      vsphere_copy:
        hostname: "{{ vcenter_hostname }}"
        username: "{{ vcenter_username }}"
        password: "{{ vcenter_password }}"
        validate_certs: "{{ vcenter_validate_certs }}"
```

```
datacenter: "{{ vcenter_datacenter }}"
datastore: "{{ vcenter_datastore }}"
src: "{{ mysrc }}"
path: "{{ mydest }}"
```

The vars.yml file stores all the VMware infrastructure connection parameters that may be shared among different Ansible Playbook files.

- vars.yml

```
---
vcenter_hostname: "vmware.example.com"
vcenter_datacenter: "vmwaredatacenter"
vcenter_validate_certs: false
vcenter_username: "username@vsphere.local"
vcenter_password: "MySecretPassword123"
vcenter_datastore: "Datastore"
```

The Ansible inventory is only the localhost because you're executing the Ansible automation on the Ansible controller.

- Inventory

  localhost

A successful execution output includes

- Target host: localhost

- Command result: ok=2 changed=1

- Return value:

```
TASK [copy file to datastore]
changed: [localhost]
```

An unsuccessful execution output specifies the reason why it fails. In the following example, the source file iso/ubuntu-22.04-live-server-amd64.iso is not available in the Automation Controller file system.

- Target host: localhost

- Command result: failed=1

- Return value:

```
TASK [copy file to datastore]
fatal: [localhost]: FAILED! => {"changed": false, "msg":
"Failed to open src file [Errno 2] No such file or
directory: 'iso/ubuntu-22.04-live-server-amd64.iso'"}
```

You can see the result of the uploading of the file to the VMware vSphere datastore in the VMware vSphere web user interface. You can find this information in the VMware vSphere web console, in the "Storage" area. You can browse the datastore path via the "Files" area. See Figure 3-18.

- 10 files before upload are already present in the ISO folder of the Datastore datastore.

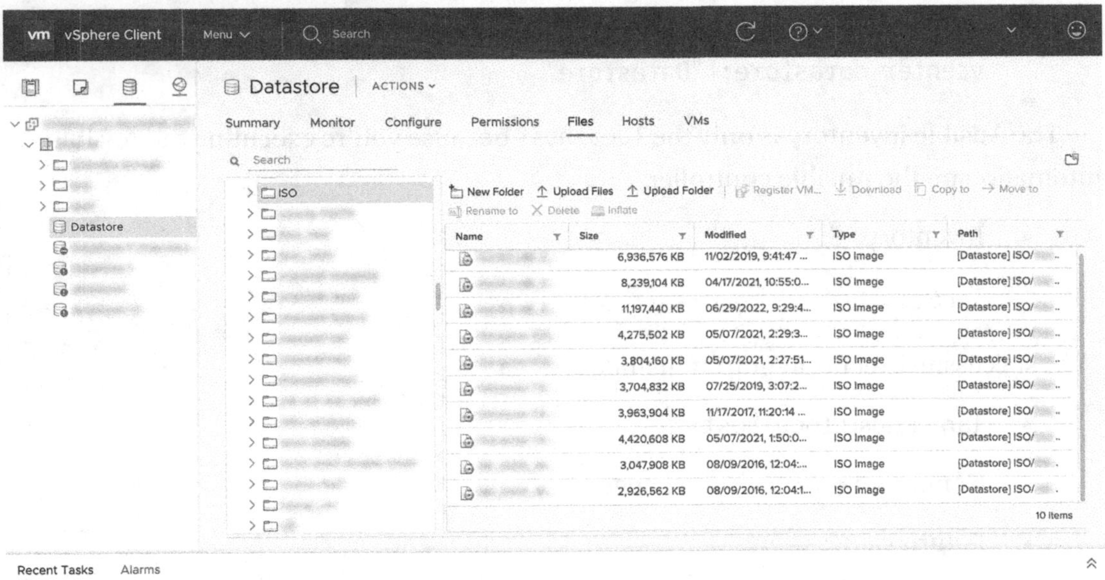

Figure 3-18. *Before uploading a file to the VMware datastore*

- 11 files are present in the ISO folder of Datastore datastore after uploading. See Figure 3-19.

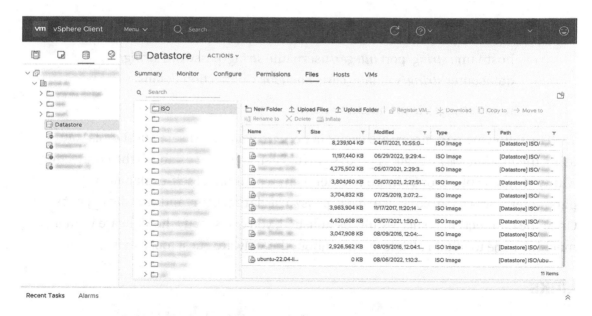

Figure 3-19. *After uploading a file to the VMware datastore*

Getting the Status of VMware Guest Tools

You can automate the gathering of the status of VMware virtual machine guest tools using an Ansible Playbook and the vmware_guest_tools_info module (see Figure 3-20). VMware guest tools are a set of services and modules that enable additional features for better performance of the guests' operating systems and seamless user interaction with VMware virtual machines. An accurate report of the current status of the VMware guest tools in your VMware virtual machines (running, not-running, up-to-date, not-installed) is crucial for a better performance of workload distribution across your VMware infrastructure.

Ansible Module vmware_guest_tools_info

- `community.vmware.vmware_guest_tools_info`

You can collect information about the status of VMware guest tools using the Ansible module vmware_guest_tools_info. The full name is community.vmware.vmware_guest_tools_info, which means that it is part of the collection of modules that interact with VMware and is community supported. The module's purpose is to gather information about VMware guest tools installed in a VMware virtual machine.

Parameters

- hostname *string*/port *integer*/username *string*/password *string*/ datacenter *string*/validate_certs *boolean*: Connection details

- name *string*: Virtual machine name

The following parameters are useful in order to get the VMware guest tools status using the module vmware_guest_tools_info. First, you must establish the connection with VMware vSphere or VMware vCenter using a plethora of self-explanatory parameters: hostname, port, username, password, datacenter, and validate_certs. Once the connection is successfully established, you can specify the VMware virtual machine name to obtain all information about the VMware guest tools on it.

Links

- community.vmware.vmware_guest_tools_info, https://docs. ansible.com/ansible/latest/collections/community/vmware/ vmware_guest_tools_info_module.html

Code

I'm going to show you how to gather information about a specific myvm VMware virtual machine and select the running host using an Ansible Playbook (see Figure 3-20). The Ansible Playbook includes the file vars.yml for some common variables for the VMware infrastructure and has two tasks. The first task acquires information from the myvm VMware virtual machine and saves the result in the vmtools_info Ansible variable. The second task prints onscreen the values of the vmtools_info Ansible variable using the debug Ansible module. Under the hood, Ansible interacts with the VMware API via Python libraries to execute the operation and verify the successful startup of the virtual machine.

- vm_guest_tools_info.yml

```
---

- name: vmware guest tools info demo
  hosts: localhost

  gather_facts: false
  collections:
```

```
    - community.vmware
  pre_tasks:
    - include_vars: vars.yml
  tasks:
    - name: guest tools info
      vmware_guest:
        hostname: "{{ vcenter_hostname }}"
        username: "{{ vcenter_username }}"
        password: "{{ vcenter_password }}"
        validate_certs: "{{ vcenter_validate_certs }}"
        datacenter: "{{ vcenter_datacenter }}"
        name: "{{ vm_name }}"
      register: vmtools_info

    - name: print guest tools info
      ansible.builtin.debug:
        var: vmtools_info
```

The vars.yml file stores all the VMware infrastructure connection parameters that may be shared among different Ansible Playbook files.

- vars.yml

```
---
vcenter_hostname: "vmware.example.com"
vcenter_datacenter: "vmwaredatacenter"
vcenter_validate_certs: false
vcenter_username: "username@vsphere.local"
vcenter_password: "MySecretPassword123"
vm_name: "myvm"
```

The Ansible inventory is only the localhost because you're executing the Ansible automation on the Ansible controller.

- Inventory

```
localhost
```

A successful execution output of virtual machine without with VMware guest tools installed Open VM Tools includes

- Target host: `localhost`

- Command result: `ok=3  changed=0`

- Return value:

```
TASK [guest tools info]
ok: [localhost]
TASK [print guest tools info]
ok: [localhost] => {
    "vmtools_info": {
        "changed": false,
        "failed": false,
        "vmtools_info": {
            "vm_name": "myvm",
            "vm_tools_install_status": "toolsOk",
            "vm_tools_install_type": "guestToolsTypeOpenVMTools",
            "vm_tools_last_install_count": 0,
            "vm_tools_running_status": "guestToolsRunning",
            "vm_tools_upgrade_policy": "manual",
            "vm_tools_version": 10282,
            "vm_tools_version_status": "guestToolsUnmanaged",
        }
    }
}
```

In this case, the VMware virtual machine `myvm` VMware guest tools status is

- VMware guest tools installed (`"vm_tools_version_status"`: `"toolsOk"`)

- VMware guest tools running (`"vm_tools_running_status"`: `"guestToolsRunning"`)

- VMware guest tools type OpenVM ("vm_tools_install_type": "guestToolsTypeOpenVMTools")

- VMware guest tools upgrade policy manual ("vm_tools_upgrade_policy": "manual")

A successful execution output of virtual machine without VMware guest tools output includes

- Target host: localhost

- Command result: ok=3 changed=0

- Return value:

```
TASK [guest tools info]
ok: [localhost]
TASK [print guest tools info]
ok: [localhost] => {
    "vmtools_info": {
        "changed": false,
        "failed": false,
        "vmtools_info": {
            "vm_name": "myvm",
            "vm_tools_install_status": "toolsNotInstalled",
            "vm_tools_install_type": "guestToolsTypeUnknown",
            "vm_tools_last_install_count": 0,
            "vm_tools_running_status": "guestToolsNotRunning",
            "vm_tools_upgrade_policy": "manual",
            "vm_tools_version": 0,
            "vm_tools_version_status": "guestToolsNotInstalled",
        }
    }
}
```

In this case, the VMware virtual machine `myvm` VMware guest tools status is

- VMware guest tools NOT installed (`"vm_tools_version_status"`: `"guestToolsNotInstalled"`)

- VMware guest tools NOT running (`"vm_tools_running_status"`: `"guestToolsNotRunning"`)

- VMware guest tools upgrade policy manual (`"vm_tools_upgrade_policy"`: `"manual"`)

You can see the result of the gathering of the status of the VMware guest tools of a specific virtual machine in the VMware vSphere web user interface in the "VMware Tools" field on the Summary page. See Figure 3-20.

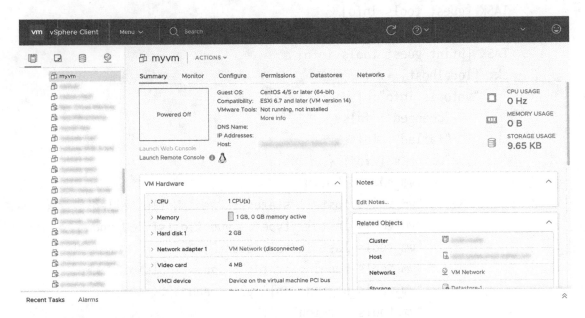

Figure 3-20. *VMware guest tools status in VMware vSphere web UI*

Upgrading VMware Guest Tools

You can automate the upgrade of the VMware virtual machine guest tools using an Ansible Playbook and the `vmware_guest_tools_upgrade` module (see Figure 3-21 for before the execution and Figure 3-22 for after the execution). Maintaining up-to-date VMware guest tools is a good practice to obtain the best performance from your VMware virtual machines. The upgrade procedure supports the VMware guest tools and the Open VM tools (`open-vm-tools`, the open source implementation for Linux guest operating systems).

Ansible Module vmware_guest_tools_upgrade

- `community.vmware.vmware_guest_tools_upgrade`

You can collect information about a VMware datastore using the Ansible module `vmware_guest_tools_upgrade`. The full name is `community.vmware.vmware_guest_tools_upgrade`, which means that it is part of the collection of modules that interact with VMware and is community supported. The module's purpose is to smoothly upgrade the VMware guest tools installed in a VMware virtual machine.

Parameters

- hostname *string*/port *integer*/username *string*/password *string*/ datacenter *string*/validate_certs *boolean*: Connection details

- name *string*: Virtual machine name

The following parameters are useful in order to upgrade the VMware guest tools using the module `vmware_datastore_info`. First, you must to establish the connection with VMware vSphere or VMware vCenter using a plethora of self-explanatory parameters: `hostname`, `port`, `username`, `password`, `datacenter`, and `validate_certs`. Once the connection is successfully established, you can specify the VMware virtual machine `name` to obtain all of the information about the VMware guest tools on it.

Links

- `community.vmware.vmware_guest_tools_upgrade`, `https://docs.ansible.com/ansible/latest/collections/community/vmware/vmware_guest_tools_upgrade_module.html`

Code

I'm going to show you how to upgrade guest tools for the `myvm` VMware virtual machine. The Ansible Playbook includes the file `vars.yml` for common variables for the VMware infrastructure and has five tasks. The first task ensures the `myvm` VMware virtual machine is powered on. The second task acquires the UUID of the `myvm` VMware virtual machine and saves the result in the `detailed_vm_info` Ansible variable. The third task executes the VMware guest tools upgrade consuming the `detailed_vm_info.instance.hw_product_uuid` Ansible variable (see "Getting a VMware Virtual Machine UUID" section). The fourth task obtains the updated VMware guest tools information and saves it in the `vmtools_info` Ansible variable. The last task prints onscreen the values of the `vmtools_info` Ansible variable using the debug Ansible module. Under the hood, Ansible interacts with the VMware API via Python libraries to execute the operation and verify the successful startup of the virtual machine.

- `vm_guest_tools_upgrade.yml`

```
---
- name: vmware guest tools upgrade demo
  hosts: localhost
  gather_facts: false
  collections:
    - community.vmware
  pre_tasks:
    - include_vars: vars.yml
  tasks:
    - name: VM powered-on
      vmware_guest_powerstate:
        hostname: "{{ vcenter_hostname }}"
        username: "{{ vcenter_username }}"
        password: "{{ vcenter_password }}"
        validate_certs: "{{ vcenter_validate_certs }}"
        name: "{{ vm_name }}"
        state: powered-on

    - name: VM get UUID
      vmware_guest_info:
        hostname: "{{ vcenter_hostname }}"
        username: "{{ vcenter_username }}"
        password: "{{ vcenter_password }}"
        datacenter: "{{ vcenter_datacenter }}"
        validate_certs: "{{ vcenter_validate_certs }}"
```

```
        name: "{{ vm_name }}"
      register: detailed_vm_info

  - name: vmware guest tools upgrade
    vmware_guest_tools_upgrade:
      hostname: "{{ vcenter_hostname }}"
      username: "{{ vcenter_username }}"
      password: "{{ vcenter_password }}"
      validate_certs: "{{ vcenter_validate_certs }}"
      datacenter: "{{ vcenter_datacenter }}"
      uuid: "{{ detailed_vm_info.instance.hw_product_uuid }}"

  - name: guest tools info
    vmware_guest_tools_info:
      hostname: "{{ vcenter_hostname }}"
      username: "{{ vcenter_username }}"
      password: "{{ vcenter_password }}"
      validate_certs: "{{ vcenter_validate_certs }}"
      datacenter: "{{ vcenter_datacenter }}"
      name: "{{ vm_name }}"
    register: vmtools_info

  - name: print guest tools info
    ansible.builtin.debug:
      var: vmtools_info
```

The vars.yml file stores all the VMware infrastructure connection parameters that may be shared among different Ansible Playbook files.

- vars.yml

```
---
vcenter_hostname: "vmware.example.com"
vcenter_datacenter: "vmwaredatacenter"
vcenter_validate_certs: false
vcenter_username: "username@vsphere.local"
vcenter_password: "MySecretPassword123"
vm_name: "myvm"
```

The Ansible inventory is only the `localhost` because you're executing the Ansible automation on the Ansible controller.

- Inventory

  `localhost`

A successful execution output includes

- Target host: `localhost`

- Command result: `ok=6 changed=1`

- Return value:

```
TASK [VM powered-on]
ok: [localhost]
TASK [VM get UUID]
ok: [localhost]
TASK [vmware guest tools upgrade]
changed: [localhost]
TASK[guest tools info]
ok: [localhost]
TASK[print guest tools info]
ok: [localhost] => {
    "vmtools_info": {
        "changed": false,
        "failed": false,
        "vmtools_info": {
            "vm_name": "myvm",
            "vm_tools_install_status": "toolsOk",
            "vm_tools_install_type": "guestToolsTypeOpenVMTools",
            "vm_tools_last_install_count": 0,
            "vm_tools_running_status": "guestToolsRunning",
            "vm_tools_upgrade_policy": "manual",
            "vm_tools_version": 10282,
            "vm_tools_version_status": "guestToolsUnmanaged",
        }
    }
}
```

After the execution, the VMware virtual machine myvm VMware guest tools status is

- VMware guest tools installed ("vm_tools_version_status": "toolsOk")

- VMware guest tools running ("vm_tools_running_status": "guestToolsRunning")

- VMware guest tools type OpenVM ("vm_tools_install_type": "guestToolsTypeOpenVMTools")

Please note that VMware guest tools must successfully be installed to be able to successfully upgrade them. An unsuccessful execution output includes a fatal error message:

- Target host: localhost

- Command result: ok=3 failed=1

- Return value:

```
TASK [VM powered-on]
ok: [localhost]
TASK [VM get UUID]
ok: [localhost]
TASK [vmware guest tools upgrade]
fatal: [localhost]: FAILED! => {"changed": false, "msg": "VMware
tools is either not running or not installed"}
```

You can see the result of the upgrade of the VMware virtual machine guest tools of a specific virtual machine in the VMware vSphere Web user interface in the "VMware Tools" field on the Summary page. See Figures 3-21 and 3-22.

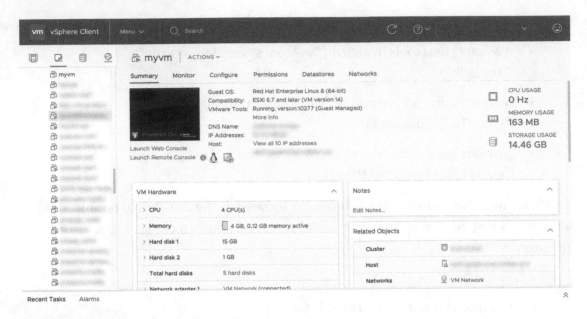

Figure 3-21. *Before the VMware guest tools upgrade in the VMware vSphere web UI*

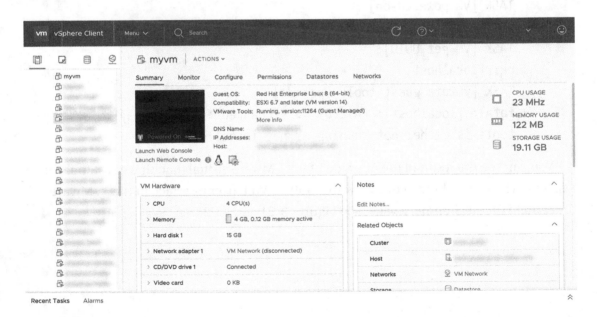

Figure 3-22. *After the VMware guest tools upgrade in the VMware vSphere web UI*

Live Migration of a VMware Virtual Machine Using vMotion

You can automate the live migration of a VMware virtual machine guest using VMware vMotion, an Ansible Playbook, and the `vmware_vmotion` module (see Figure 3-23 for before the execution and Figure 3-24 for after the execution). The VMware vMotion technology allows zero-downtime live migration of a VMware virtual machine. Combined with VMware vSphere Storage vMotion, you can achieve this across vSwitches, clusters, and even clouds (depending on your VMware license). This is a great feature for mission-critical business continuity resources. Ansible is able to take advantage of VMware vMotion and enable more automation scenarios in your VMware infrastructure with the `vmware_vmotion` module. For example, you can systematically move resources to power down hosts or provide better resource allocation.

Ansible vmware_vmotion Module

- `community.vmware.vmware_vmotion`

The Ansible module `vmware_vmotion` is used to move VMware virtual machines in your VMware infrastructure using VMware vMotion technology. The full name is `community.vmware.vmware_vmotion`, which means that it is part of the collection of modules that interact with VMware and is community supported. The module's purpose is to move a virtual machine using vMotion.

Parameters

- hostname *string*/port *integer*/username *string*/password *string*/ datacenter *string*/validate_certs *boolean*: Connection details

- destination_host *string*: Destination VMware host

- destination_datastore *string*: Destination VMware datastore

- destination_datacenter *string*: Destination VMware datacenter

- destination_cluster *string*: Destination VMware cluster

- destination_resourcepool *string*: Destination VMware resource pool

- destination_datastore_cluster *string*: Destination VMware datastore cluster (storage pod)

The following parameters are useful in order to live migrate a VMware virtual machine using vMotion using the module vmware_vmotion. First, you must establish the connection with VMware vSphere or VMware vCenter using a plethora of self-explanatory parameters: hostname, port, username, password, datacenter, and validate_certs.

Once the connection is successfully established, you can specify if you want only to change the VMware host destination_host (VMware host vMotion) or also change the storage with destination_datastore (VMware storage vMotion). More complex scenarios can be specified using destination_datacenter, destination_cluster, destination_resourcepool, and destination_datastore_cluster.

Links

- community.vmware.vmware_vmotion, https://docs.ansible.com/ansible/latest/collections/community/vmware/vmware_vmotion_module.html

Code

I'm going to show you how to move the VMware virtual machine myvm from the host host1.vmware.example.com to the host host2.vmware.example.com using an Ansible Playbook (see Figure 3-23 for before the execution and Figure 3-24 for after the execution). The Ansible Playbook includes the file vars.yml for common variables for the VMware Infrastructure and has two tasks. The first task performs the moving operation on the myvm VMware virtual machine and saves the result in the vm_info Ansible variable. The second task prints onscreen the values of the vm_info.running_host Ansible variable. For more information, refer to the section "Getting a VMware Virtual Machine Running Host". Under the hood, Ansible interacts with the VMware API via Python libraries to execute the operation and verify the successful startup of the virtual machine.

- vm_vmotion.yml

```
---

- name: vm vmotion demo
  hosts: localhost

  gather_facts: false
```

```
vars:
  destination_host: "host2.vmware.example.com"
collections:
  - community.vmware
pre_tasks:
  - include_vars: vars.yml
tasks:
  - name: VM vmotion
    vmware_vmotion:
      hostname: "{{ vcenter_hostname }}"
      username: "{{ vcenter_username }}"
      password: "{{ vcenter_password }}"
      validate_certs: "{{ vcenter_validate_certs }}"
      vm_name: "{{ vm_name }}"
      destination_host: "{{ destination_host }}"
    register: vm_info

  - name: VM running host
    ansible.builtin.debug:
      var: vm_info.running_host
```

The vars.yml file stores all the VMware infrastructure connection parameters that may be shared among different Ansible Playbook files.

- vars.yml

```
---
vcenter_hostname: "vmware.example.com"
vcenter_datacenter: "vmwaredatacenter"
vcenter_validate_certs: false
vcenter_username: "username@vsphere.local"
vcenter_password: "MySecretPassword123"
vm_name: "myvm"
```

The Ansible inventory is only the localhost because you're executing the Ansible automation on the Ansible controller.

- Inventory

```
localhost
```

A successful execution output includes

- Target host: `localhost`

- Command result: `ok=3 changed=1`

- Return value:

```
TASK [VM vmotion]
changed: [localhost]
TASK [VM running host]
ok: [localhost] => {
    "vm_info.running_host": "host2.vmware.example.com"
}
```

If the virtual machine is not compatible with the VMware format on the target host, the module returns the following status:

- Target host: `localhost`

- Command result: `ok=1 failed=1`

- Return value:

```
TASK [VM vmotio]
fatal: [localhost]: FAILED! => {"changed": false, "msg":
"(\"The virtual machine version is not compatible with the
version of the host 'host2.vmware.example.com'.\", None)"}
```

After the execution of the code, you expect the following result in your VMware vSphere client user interface in the "Host" field on the Summary page. See Figures 3-23 and 3-24.

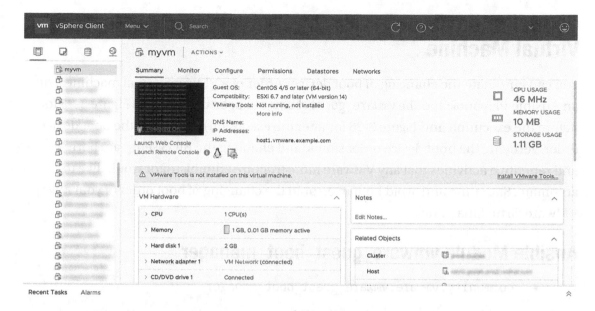

Figure 3-23. *Before moving the VMware virtual machine*

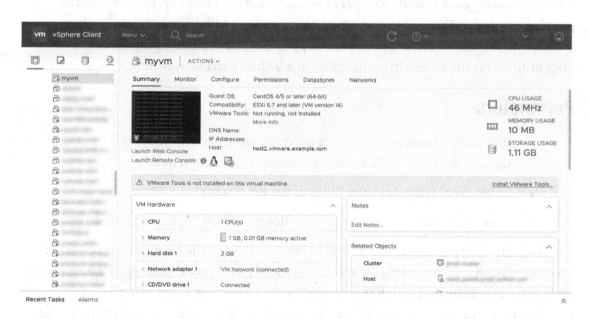

Figure 3-24. *After moving the VMware virtual machine*

Changing the Boot Device Order of a VMware Virtual Machine

You can automate the changing of boot devices order of a VMware virtual machine using an Ansible Playbook and the `vmware_guest_boot_manager` module (see Figure 3-25 for before the execution and Figure 3-26 for after the execution). Changing the boot devices order, verifying the boot device order status, and enabling the BIOS setup are boring and repetitive activities that any VMware infrastructure administrator would like to automate. Save time and avoid human error in the changing of boot order of your `myvm` VMware virtual machine.

Ansible Module vmware_guest_boot_manager

- `community.vmware.vmware_guest_boot_manager`

You can collect information about the VMware guest tools status using the Ansible module `vmware_guest_boot_manager`. The full name is `community.vmware.vmware_guest_boot_manager`, which means that it is part of the collection of modules that interact with VMware and is community supported. The module's purpose is to manage boot options for the given virtual machine in a VMware virtual machine.

Parameters

- hostname *string*/port *integer*/username *string*/password *string*/ datacenter *string*/validate_certs *boolean*: Connection details

- enter_bios_setup *boolean*: Enter in the BIOS setup

- boot_order *list*: Boot devices order (floppy, CD-ROM, Ethernet, disk)

The following parameters are useful in order to change the boot devices order of a VMware virtual machine using the module `vmware_guest_boot_manager`. First, you must establish the connection with VMware vSphere or VMware vCenter using a plethora of self-explanatory parameters: `hostname`, `port`, `username`, `password`, `datacenter`, and `validate_certs`.

Once the connection is successfully established, you can enable entering the BIOS setup using the `enter_bios_setup` boolean and the boot devices order via the `boot_order` list, such as floppy, CD-ROM, Ethernet, and disk. The system will try to boot from the order of the specified devices.

Code

The Ansible Playbook includes the file `vars.yml` for common variables for the VMware Infrastructure and has one task. Under the hood, Ansible interacts with the VMware API via Python libraries to execute the operation and verify the successful startup of the virtual machine.

- `vm_change_boot.yml`

```yaml
---
- name: vm change book demo
  hosts: localhost

  gather_facts: false
  collections:
    - community.vmware
  pre_tasks:
    - include_vars: vars.yml
  tasks:
    - name: VM change boot order
      vmware_guest_boot_manager:
        hostname: "{{ vcenter_hostname }}"
        username: "{{ vcenter_username }}"
        password: "{{ vcenter_password }}"
        validate_certs: "{{ vcenter_validate_certs }}"
        name: "{{ vm_name }}"
        enter_bios_setup: true
        boot_order:
          - cdrom
          - disk
          - ethernet
```

The `vars.yml` file stores all the VMware infrastructure connection parameters that may be shared among different Ansible Playbook files.

- vars.yml

```
---
vcenter_hostname: "vmware.example.com"
vcenter_datacenter: "vmwaredatacenter"
vcenter_validate_certs: false
vcenter_username: "username@vsphere.local"
vcenter_password: "MySecretPassword123"
vm_name: "myvm"
```

The Ansible inventory is only the localhost because you're executing the Ansible automation on the Ansible controller.

- Inventory

  localhost

A successful execution output includes

- Target host: localhost

- Command result: ok=1 changed=1

- Return value:

  ```
  TASK [VM change boot order]
  changed: [localhost]
  ```

The execution of this code is idempotent.

You can see the result of changing the boot order in the BIOS setup of a VMware virtual machine in the VMware vSphere web user interface using the web/remote console. See Figures 3-25 and 3-26.

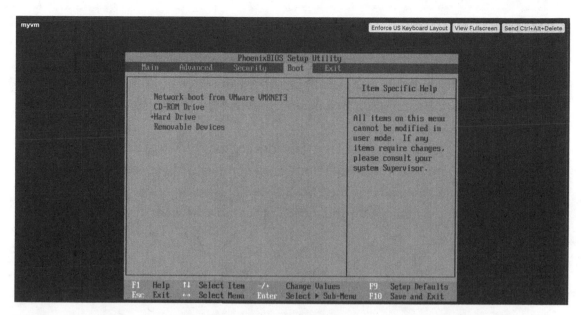

Figure 3-25. *Before changing the boot order of the VMware virtual machine*

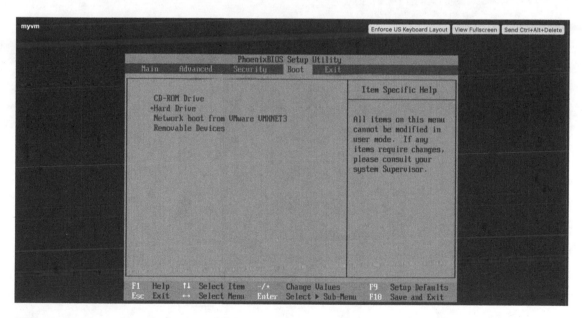

Figure 3-26. *After changing the boot order of the VMware virtual machine*

Key Takeaways

This chapter moved deeply into VMware infrastructure automation and providing some code nutshells and code sample snippets to use in your day-to-day journey. It demystified the successful setup, installation, and troubleshooting of Ansible for VMware.

Now you have a great overview of the powerful `community.vmware` collection resources that you can use to automate simple and complex VMware repetitive tasks that were previously done manually via the VMware vSphere user interface.

In the next chapter, I thank you and recap how to move forward in your Ansible automation journey.

CHAPTER 4

Closing Remarks

Please let me remind you that Ansible is an evolving open source product, so check out the Ansible official website at `www.ansible.com` for the latest news and updates.

In this book, we covered the most useful day-to-day code snippets and activities to automate your VMware infrastructure. Use this book as guidance in your day-to-day life, but also use your own creativity to invent new automation workflows.

This is where Ansible starts becoming thoroughly useful and time saving. Every day I found new ways to automate my daily tasks using Ansible and discovered new modules, plugins, and collections designed by third parties.

The number of people who contribute day after day to the Ansible project is impressive and it means they're creating a great worldwide community that communicates in the same language and shares the same ideas, opinions, problems, and solutions. The most successful enterprises and professionals are innovating their businesses in this way.

This is where this book's story ends but your journey begins. My purpose was to share with you real examples to be used every day. It was nearly impossible to include all the possible scenarios in only one book, but I've included the most frequent and generic use cases. I know you'll come up with ideas and problems that you would like to automate with Ansible. If not, just think about the most boring and repetitive task that you execute at least twice per day and find a way to automate it (coffee tasting doesn't count). You start with a simple code, obtain a minimum viable solution to refine with your team, and that will lead to an automated complex workflow. I'm excited to hear about your automation story. I believe that this is the true essence of open source in the 21st century and we need to be very proud of it. These are the kind of things that push innovation in your business and accelerate your business. Your boss is going to love it! Check out the online and local communities and events for more automation ideas.

From the depth of my heart, I wish you the best of luck. Have a bright day and let's automate more! From now on, the sky is the limit!

© Luca Berton 2023
L. Berton, *Ansible for VMware by Examples*, https://doi.org/10.1007/978-1-4842-8879-5_4

Key Takeaways

This book is a cornerstone in your journey with the Ansible platform for an information technology VMware infrastructure.

You now have a comprehensive overview of the state-of-the-art Ansible platform, its strengths, and the programming language constructs with some battle-tested code nutshells and command-line command snippets.

The Ansible platform technology evolves every day, but the concepts and main statements are stable and have long-lasting applications.

This knowledge will guide your journey to upskill yourself with Ansible and implement VMware Infrastructure as Code (IaC) using DevOps methodologies.

Index

A, B

© Luca Berton 2023
L. Berton, *Ansible for VMware by Examples*, https://doi.org/10.1007/978-1-4842-8879-5

Printed in the United States
by Baker & Taylor Publisher Services